MASTERING
Fiction
WRITING

Books by Kit Reed

MASTERING *fiction* WRITING

KIT REED

Writer's Digest Books

Cincinnati, Ohio

95 94 93 92 91   5 4 3 2 1

Library of Congress Cataloging-in-Publication Data

Reed, Kit.
   Mastering fiction writing / by Kit Reed. — 1st ed.
      p.   cm.
   "An earlier version . . . was originally published by Prentice Hall in 1982 as Story first" — T.p. verso.
   Includes index.
   ISBN 0-89879-479-X (hard cover)
   1. Fiction — Authorship.   I. Reed, Kit. Story first. II. Title.
PN3355.R44   1991
808.3 — dc20
          91-22120
          CIP

Edited by Nan Dibble
Designed by Sandy Conopeotis
Calligraphy by Don Marsh

The following page constitutes an extension of this copyright page.

for Sister Maura, SSND
with thanks

Acknowledgments

I owe particular thanks to Carl Brandt, Paul Horgan, Richard Ohmann and Joseph Reed, each of whom brought his special intelligence and talents to a critical reading of the first draft, and to William Francisco for reminding me of the link between writers and actors. I should also like to thank Carl Younger of Brandt and Brandt. I am grateful, too, to certain students of writing at Wesleyan University, who asked a great many of the questions I am trying to answer here. My special thanks go to Cheryl Sucher, David Low, Stephen Alter and Peter Blauner, Ezra Palmer, Eileen Kelly and Suzy Berne, who were my students and who have become colleagues. Their success makes me think I must be doing something right. And I do want to thank everyone at Writer's Digest Books for having the vision to see that this book is useful in spheres far wider than the classroom.

Table of Contents

Preface

I wrote this book for people who want to write fiction. Originally titled *Story First: the Writer as Insider*, it began its publishing life as a college text. It's been in use in classrooms all over the country since 1982. Still, the best letters about the book came from the people I most wanted to reach — writers working on their own. I also heard from entirely too many teachers who kept the book in their desks and handed out my suggestions second hand, when I most wanted to reach you who are actually writing fiction. This *Writer's Digest* edition is specially designed for you. In addition to expanding on certain points, answering readers' questions, I've added sets of questions to help you get the best out of your own writing. Most important, this new, expanded and updated edition gives me the opportunity to include everything I've learned in the course of writing fiction and working with student fiction writers over the years since I first wrote it.

When I was little and wanted to grow up to be a writer, I imagined writing as a series of tricks or secrets grownups knew. All I had to do was find out what they were and master them. Then I too could be A Writer.

Because I believed in books I thought there must be a book somewhere that would give me all the answers. All I had to do was find this book and bring it home from the store and go through it, chapter by chapter. I would follow the directions, step by step, and when I had done all this I would automatically bridge the gap between my books and stories, hand-lettered on notebook paper, and the books I had read and loved from the moment I first discovered them.

Even after I was old enough to know better, I cherished the idea that there were easy answers waiting for me somewhere. I knew by that time just how hard writing was, and because I did, I could not shake the hope that I could shortcut or escape some of the more painful parts of the process by picking up certain tricks of the trade. As a reporter who wanted to be a writer, I worked overtime to stage interviews with novelists. I asked questions relentlessly and took notes. I studied their life stories for details and looked for lessons in the clothes they wore and the way their desk tops were arranged because I thought that somewhere amid the externals I might find some of the answers.

Several million words and a few busted novels later I understood that there weren't any answers. There were never any tricks because writing is not a finite business, it is process, and the process continues for as long as a writer writes. Writers can and do get better at what they are doing but there is always that perfect story or novel shimmering just out of reach. As long as they live there is always that extra mile to go. I discovered that there wasn't any one book, either, but by the time I understood all these things I had been writing for so long that it didn't matter to me; I was never going to stop. I might never know everything about what I was doing or hoped to do, but I had learned about some of this and would never stop learning.

Writing is learned on the job and the real teacher is experience.

Around the time I understood this and understood it fully, I was asked to teach. I found myself involved with would-be writers who seemed to think that because I had been around for a few years, several novels and a few dozen stories, I might have something to tell them. In the course of trying to explain to students why one story worked and another didn't, I was forced to examine and explain what up until then had been a basically private and instinctive process. Teaching, I did not learn any more about how to do what I was doing, but I was pressed to explain how I did it.

I don't think anybody can teach anybody else how to write, but if somebody is already disposed to write then it may be possible for a second party to help the beginning writer be a little better at it. The classroom may be the last place in which a would-be writer is asked to write. There are regular assignments. There is an audience. The demands of the class impose the discipline, and discussions help writers go the distance between what they have on the page and what they intend. In the classroom as teacher, I found myself wishing once again for that book: not to help me write, but to help me to teach writing.

This is an attempt at that book. I have tried to describe as simply as possible the process of making fiction as I have begun to understand it through writing, and through trying to talk to beginning writers about writing.

Because this is a book about process rather than product, I will not devote any chapters to "theme," or Big Ideas, or any of the intellectual elements that so many critics like to extract from fiction, or attach to it *from the outside*. I believe these are elements a reader may be interested in as he dissects a finished story, and not items to be taken off a shelf by a writer making a work of fiction. I believe the significance of a work comes from inside it, and that it emerges in process.

I am immediately suspicious of writers who say they are going to write a story or novel from an exclusively intellectual premise. I think most good fiction begins with people: the writer and the characters, who they are, what they *want*, and that the best fictional characters are compelled by some of the same impulses that drive their creators. If they are drawn truly, then these characters will in one way or another reflect the writer's preoccupations. A writer who sets out to clothe a set of intellectual premises in fiction will end up with a collection of department-store dummies propped in various attitudes, or else will lop arms and legs off living characters to make them fit the premise, leaving them too maimed to function. If the characters don't function the story won't either, and that Big Idea, whatever it is, is going to die aborning.

Beginning writers who have learned to look for these things as readers are too often inhibited by a sense of responsibility to them. Some time in the dim reaches of junior high school, they may have been instructed that every work of fiction worth its salt had a theme, and the implication was that the bones, heart and blood of a work of fiction were as nothing in relation to this textbook concept of a maxim or moral which could be extracted from the work, reduced to a few words and neatly labeled. They will talk about theme as a separable element, almost as if themes could be bought at the drugstore like fancy decals and glued to the outside of a story to give it significance. Others believe stories are only vehicles for Big Ideas, and all they have to do is find Ideas big enough to get their stories rolling.

Even the more sophisticated beginners will talk of plot and character and style as if they were individual items, different kinds of blocks which have to be accumulated — one of each, coming to the conclusion that the heap they make will be a story.

For the writer in the act, I think, plot, character, style, themes are inseparable parts of something that — when it works right — grows almost organically. It is easy enough for a reader to stand off from a work of fiction and make statements about the various elements, but I think these are an outsider's judgments made *after the fact*.

I believe you as writer need to work from within the story. Even the best writers are to some extent explorers of *terra incognita*, finding their way through a developmental process of trial and error. Once the discoveries are made, they seem beautiful and so logical and right that the reader may think the visible pattern was there first, and the story hung itself on it. More often than not, the pattern is, rather, the visible result of something I call "inner logic," which is, simply, the set of rules each story makes for itself. It determines what can and ultimately will happen within a particular fictional framework. If it is sound, and if you as writer test and discard and make choices according to *what is right for this particular story*, then the rest, matter and manner, will emerge because they were implicit in that particular work when you as writer began the story and you needed only to discover and try to perfect the inner logic to see them develop naturally.

Until you begin writing fiction, you will continue to know the elements of fiction only intellectually and from the outside. As a writer you need to know them more or less instinctively, from having read as much fiction as you can. You need to feed on shapes and impressions and means of expression in some of the same ways that a small child feeds on words, so that you will in the end learn to write in the same natural way that you learned to talk. Nobody sat down and taught you to speak your native language; you learned by listening and then trying a few words. Immersed in reading fiction, you are going to try to write a few words yourself — a few hundred thousand words.

If I stress the idea of learning to write fiction from the inside, as writer rather than as reader/critic, it is because I think a writer making fiction needs to treat every decision made and every element chosen for a story as brand new. This does not mean that design and intention are absent from real fiction, or that fiction has to be devoid of ideas. It means, rather, that I believe these things should and will develop within the story, which comes from inside the writer. They will develop in process, and emerge as the story emerges. The story comes first.

As a writer engaged in a lifetime of trial and error and discovery, I cannot offer you any clear-cut set of instructions, nor can I give you The Answers, or even tell you which are The Answers for you. I offer instead a partial map of what is essentially *terra incognita*, made by somebody who has been there, and designed for people who are going to make that first exploratory voyage, who are going to make it in spite of anything I might say or do to dissuade them.

—K.R.
Middletown, Connecticut

Sources: Where I Think Fiction Comes From

*B*eginning to write fiction, you may wonder what you have to write about. Even a young writer has plenty of material stored. The problem is not where to find it, but how to get at it.

A writer begins by learning to identify stored material. This means being willing and ready to remember, to add to memory through observation, and to make sense of what is observed and remembered through a habit of self-examination that is part of writing for as long as the writer lives and works. Add to this the complex and rewarding process that makes the writer of fiction a writer of fiction and not a diarist or a journalist or historian. I call it transformation. Transforming the raw materials, the writer attempts to order all the profusion and disorder of life, taking whatever comes to hand to make something new: a work of fiction.

What are the raw materials? As writer, you can draw on everything you have seen or heard or learned and everything that's ever happened to you. You have as well everything you've ever felt or read or comprehended or failed to comprehend. All these elements have been sifting into your memory over the years, accumulating in an alluvial sludge somewhere at the back of your consciousness. It's there now, growing richer as you grow older. If you are willing to start wading around in this sludge, you will discover how rich you are.

At one point my resident critic asked me where I'd picked up a song I was singing. I said, "On memory lane." Then I looked him in the eye and said, "I'm strip mining it."

Look into memory. You have your past to draw on: family, or lack of family; relationships within the family, with friends, with enemies. There are the places you have been or want to go, from Middletown to Marrakesh; there are all the people you have met or heard about or seen or overheard. Once you have recognized all these sources you can number another: the world you are living in. You are very much a product of your own country, your particular corner of the culture with its quirks and cadences, and your perceptions are informed or affected by a new element: the rapidly developing global consciousness. As a writer, you have the singular distinction of being yourself, at your age, in this last decade of the twentieth century, when for the first time it is possible for everybody to know, all at once, whenever a volcano erupts or a new government comes to power, to watch revolutions and assassinations live and in color. You are not stuffed in a garret somewhere, writing in a vacuum. Like it or not, you are in touch with the rest of the world in a way that is unique to this generation of writers. It is bound to affect your writing.

You will enrich your holdings through observation. Observation begins with intense curiosity about anything and everything. You need to be willing to look at everything new and to examine old things as if they were new: familiar faces, rooms, landscapes. Most writers I know are madly visual. They can tell you almost everything about somebody else's parlor. They will notice if a single object in your house has been moved or added, and if you ask them what a third person looks like they will delight in telling you, with gestures, picking out the exact details to give you the person. Most writers are insatiable eavesdroppers, storing up good lines the way other people save string. They're listening for cadences, too, and when they tell stories at parties they can usually do all the voices, reproducing accents and character walks.

The people you observe have more than external detail to give you. They all have stories, and most of them love to tell them. As you listen you will learn to read life like a novel. Collecting the life stories that abound everywhere, projecting on what you have gathered, you will be able to invent new ones, imagining scenes where you were never present, unfolding in places you've never been.

At a deeper level, observation means learning people from the inside, developing your perceptions, or sensitivity, to a point where you can begin to have a fair idea of what they are thinking. This means listening not only to what they are telling you but also to what they are trying to tell you, or trying to keep from you, being aware of their feelings and alert to the discrepancies between what they mean to do and what they end up doing. This is not to record their responses on tape for storage so you can regurgitate them later. It is, rather, so you can begin to understand them. Understanding, you will try to imagine *what you would do if you were a particular person in a given situation.*

I do not believe in writing unvarnished autobiography, or even writing directly from life, so that only the names are changed to protect the innocent. I think it is sometimes unscrupulous and always self-limiting. The writer who uses up the childhood in a first novel and the rotten first marriage in a second will have to live through a new crisis before he can write another. The writer who uses up the life stories of those around him may end up in court, or in trouble, and even if nobody sues or complains, this writer is also limited, because part of the process of making fiction is learning to shape and make sense of raw happening, and part of the pleasure is making something *more* than what already is.

Observe, then, collect, let the bits and pieces sink into that alluvial sludge and stay there until the whole mixture grows richer. When you draw on them again the bits and pieces will emerge as brand new — yours, and no one else's.

Writers who collect and assimilate in this way are never bored because they are engaged in an unending process of collecting, embroidering, projecting. They love detail, they love speculation and they are often as good at diagnosis and analysis as any trained psychologist. They are eavesdroppers and pack rats and, I suppose, thieves, taking little bits of other people's lives from them so deftly that they won't even know they are missing. Then, because they are voracious and unscrupulous, they'll use those fragments as cavalierly as if they were their own. Most writers are working even when they look as if they're doing something else. They're considering, sifting, assimilating what they have taken until the bits and pieces are ready to emerge as fiction. They are also accomplished liars, taking what really happened and turning it into something *more* than it was; they can say what they want about life and use every trick in the book to make you believe it.

The writer is rich, no matter what the external circumstances. The bill collectors and the burglars may come and take away everything in the house, but when the jewelry and the car and the furniture are all gone the writer's secret hoard is still intact. The impoverished writer can be discovered in an empty room as happy as any pack rat, surrounded by what would look like junk to the rest of the world but what is, indeed, a fabulous collection, bottles and old magazines and snapshots and bits of string and tough moments and captured glances, all the bits and pieces discovered and laid by because sooner or later they may come in handy.

Look what you've already collected:

1. An entire childhood, happy or unhappy.
2. Inside knowledge of parents or guardians or institutions you grew up with.
3. Knowledge of attitudes, customs, quirks of the people you grew up with — from family or friends to the larger society.
4. Close knowledge of local geography — terrain, from the color of earth to what grows there to the kinds of fast food stands along the nearest superhighway.
5. Everything good that's every happened to you, from falling in love to getting a first job to raising a family.
6. Everything bad that's ever happpened to you, from deaths in the family to loss of friends, separation from spouse or lover.
7. Daily business: jobs you've held, occupations or professions you know as an insider or an observer; how the town or city you live in operates, either at the official or the personal level.

This is only a beginning. The items on your own list will number in the hundreds, perhaps the thousands.

Collecting is easy and fun. The rest of the job is complex at best, and often painful. It is self-examination, or introspection. A writer has to be willing to look inside, to explore and investigate, to pry up scabs and probe old hurts and examine motives. A writer must be willing to look at everything, from unexpressed fears and darker wishes down to the time, all those years ago, when his mother hit him and he kicked the dog.

The process of self-examination functions at two levels. The first is a simple, workmanlike level. You must learn yourself as you attempt to learn other people, so that writing about characters, you can *become* them. Becoming characters, you will know in your bones what they are going to do in situations you create for them. You have to be able to project lives for them and make your readers believe, not that this happened, on this particular day, but that *this is precisely what would have happened*, it is the only thing that could happen in a given circumstance.

The second level is much more complex. You must know yourself in such a way that eventually you will discover your central material. I'm convinced that by the time we are grown up our books already exist within us; they are the sum of our concerns and experiences and individual vision, and they are stamped in our consciousness. Examining ourselves, and writing, we discover what we have to write about.

Identifying Your Material

This is an unending and mysterious procsss, and to try to analyze or explain it is as dangerous as attempting brain surgery with a machete. Let me say that it exists, it is individual and intensely personal; it is essential. The point of departure may be memory, but to it you must bring the will to reflect and analyze. Every writer is engaged in this process and anybody who wants to write must be willing to court this particular awareness, and with it, vulnerability. Exploring yourself, you will find your own way of looking at life and making sense of what you see; if you care to probe you may discover what makes you want to write and why, and why your best writing will be yours alone, like no one else's, as distinctive as a fingerprint.

As you discover your raw materials, you will need to learn how to transform them. I stress transformation because it is this that separates the writer of fiction from the diarist, the journalist and the historian. Instead of laying out events exactly as they happened, using up your autobiography faster than you can live it, you need to learn how to draw on everything you know and everything you are to give authenticity to the story you are making.

As a writer making fiction, I am quick to point out that I didn't make it all up. I am not making something out of nothing, which may be why I hate the term "creative writing." I am well aware that I am making something out of something. My most wildly inventive stories are composed of elements I can separate or identify, even though the most informed reader couldn't do it with a miner's lamp and a map of the inside of my head. This is because nothing is as it was when it happened, or when I saw it. I will take what I have been given and make something new of it.

I can give observed elements or attributes to fictional characters of settings or situations. A pair of Nile-green corduroy trousers I never owned turned up on a character in my first novel. Another character somewhere else has borrowed a masquerade costume I once saw. I have imagined a life story for a relative who died before I was born. I find myself transforming events in a dozen different ways. Looking back at my work I can see that fictional events stand for real events in my own life, but nobody else is going to know which ones or how unless I tell them. Transforming, I can make a dozen stories out of the truth of one particular moment. Transforming enables a writer to use remembered emotion: pain, confusion, love, feelings of loss, taking everything that is known to create something the writer could not know in any other way.

The best analog may be the Stanislavsky method of acting. Method actors draw on their own experience to bring life and character to their performances. An actor about to play a bedside scene in which another dies is expected to mourn for him. He may never have been in this situation but he will dig into his own past experience for a time in which his emotions were appropriately similar. He will go back to a moment of disappointment or loss, a brush with tragedy, and retrieve his emotions and transform them into tears at this particular deathbed. An actress will draw on her own remembered pain to create and become Mary Tyrone or Blanche DuBois, whose stories may be nothing like her own. One director used shock tactics to supply emotions to a child actress who was incapable of this kind of transformation. She was supposed to cry in a scene. He told the child her dog had died and then rolled the cameras.

As you begin to write fiction you can draw on your own experience in some of the same ways, transforming, projecting where necessary. You don't have to be a hatchet murderer to write about one. At some time in your life you've had murderous feelings. Use them. We can all write about love and loss because we have experienced them in one way or another, to one degree or another. A character falling in love with a schizophrenic or losing a parent will feel some of the same kinds of love, or loss, perhaps at a higher level of intensity. Even if you are a trick rider or a lumberjack with a checkered past, what you make up is likely to be more interesting than what you have experienced directly. Certainly there are more possibilities. Transforming, you multiply them.

Transformation

Transformation is the key. Taking the raw materials of life, you as writer will make both small and large changes to turn what you know into fictional material. *Transforming*, you will learn how to turn life into fiction instead of simply recording it.

Transformation gives you power in four significant ways.

First, *it gives you power over events.* Life is basically disorganized. Events aren't always predictable and they don't unfold in an orderly way. They aren't necessarily dramatic. Even people you like are often boring. Reframing life in fiction, you're imposing order on life. You have the ability to create dramatic high points and bring events to a satisfying resolution. A student of mine who was coming to terms with an abusive father came in grinning one day: "I just murdered him." For narrative purposes, he'd given the real-life prototype, whose life was spinning on unpleasantly, a fictional counterpart who reconciled with his son on his deathbed.

Second, *transformation has the added virtue of protecting you,* as writer, even as it protects the people you're drawing on. Nobody needs to know that's really you at the center of your story about somebody who's just been fired or who's just discovered that a lover is being unfaithful. People may suspect that's your hated professional rival in the comic piece you've just written, but if you've done your job of transforming well, they won't be able to point to any single physical or background detail that will prove it. You can also protect yourself from the anger of people you want to write about, or their hurt feelings or their accusations that you've invaded their privacy. Nobody needs to know that the loser you're writing about is your best friend or the comic character you've just created is drawn from a member of your own family.

Third, *it provides new insights.* Examining life more closely, looking at it from fresh angles, trying to see it from the point of view of your characters, imagining what they think and trying to feel what they're feeling, you'll find you will develop an insider's idea of what's going on. You'll learn to see more and understand it better.

Fourth and perhaps most important, *transformation gives you power over your story.* You can turn small happenings into big events — an argument into a fistfight, a demonstration into a riot, a kiss into a full-blown romance if it serves your narrative purposes. You can make a malicious character into a murderer or victim or even turn her into a hero if you want to. You can turn a lost wallet into a missing military document or a boring car trip into a flight from freeway snipers if it will make a better story.

Transformation is more than a matter of changing names or hair color or adding false beards or funny hats to protect the innocent. It's turning what you have into something completely new.

Beginning to Transform

Let me show you how this works with a set of exercises:

1. Your parents are recently divorced and you want to get at some of the

pain this has caused you. Imagine a character who's just been orphaned.

2. You have an overbearing employer who makes life miserable for everybody in the office. What if, instead, he were a guard in the maximum security ward of a state hospital?

3. An old family friend keeps turning up at odd moments just when you've forgotten about her. There's nothing extraordinary about her or her visits, but with a slight twist the recurring visits can open up exciting possibilities. What if she's remarkably beautiful? Hideously ugly? Psychotic? What if she's a long-lost girlfriend of your father's? An old enemy of your mother's? Your real mother?

4. You want to write about a recent breakup with a Significant Other. Imagine yourself as a character whose spouse is seeing somebody else, or as a character walking in and asking your mate for a divorce. Then take your changes one step further. Changing sexes of central characters gives you an opportunity to explore the dramatic possibilities more or less protected. Perhaps more important, it's likely to give you new ways of looking at the situation.

With these examples in mind, take a look at your own life. Pick out one person you know, one place you've been or one major event that you'd like to write about.

What do you see now that you didn't see at the time?

What changes can you make to liberate yourself from fact? To enhance your story?

What becomes clear even in this simple exercise is that there are dozens of ways of looking at any situation, and dozens more to explore everything you know, exploit it and transform it into fiction.

Now it's time to begin.

If you think you want to write and your wish to do so extends beyond credit for a term or a fond fantasy about winning friends or instant fame, then you probably want to write because there are already stirrings in the alluvial sludge at the back of your brain, shapes emerging, and it is going to take your best efforts to bring them to the surface so you can deal with them and make them work for you. Be willing to bring everything you know and are to the typewriter, and to stay there until you have brought some of this to the page.

Most writers write out of a compulsion that keeps them going at all costs and against all odds — a childhood trauma, an emotional injury or cultural dislocation or felt lack; large or small, it is something that has left them feeling unfinished and compelled to try to complete themselves in their work. People with externally ordinary lives can discover this within themselves, and the discovery is made in the process.

Beginning to write, you discover what you have to write about.

Some Ways to Start

Knowing you have everything in the world to write about, you're ready to begin. If you already know what you want to do, by all means get started.

If writing fiction is new to you, you may think you need to jump start your first story. Because there's no easy way to write fiction, no certifiable and universally recognized set of steps A, B and C that guarantees success, what follows is only a suggestion. Here's a set of questions that may help you identify at least a few of the thousands of possible points of departure.

Begin by asking yourself: What do I want to write about? Do I want to start with:

1. A person? Is this somebody like me or somebody completely different? If somebody completely different, am I drawing from somebody I know? A friend? Family member? Somebody seen or remembered or imagined?

2. Someplace I've been? What kind of people live in this setting? How does the setting affect the way they think and act and behave? An example: the villagers in a tiny seaside town in Maine are completely different from city-dwellers or suburbanites. Although they're likely to know about the rest of the world through the media, their own lives are affected by:

   a. Harsh winters, e.g. long spells when everybody's snowed in.

   b. Small town life — everybody knows everybody else.

   c. Whatever supports the town, whether it's fishing or the tourist trade.

   d. Living by the ocean, which is not like living in the mountains or on the plains or even on the Atlantic coast in New Jersey or Georgia or Florida.

3. Do I want to begin with an event? If so, is it something that's happening:

   a. In the world right now? A war or a national disaster? If so, who are my characters and how is this going to affect them? Beginning with the ancient Greek poet Homer and the Trojan war, war has prompted some brilliant fiction. Contemporary examples of national events that have shaped fiction include the assassination of President John F. Kennedy, the Vietnam War and fallout from the social and cultural revolution of the Sixties.

   b. In society? Am I trying to get to the truth behind something I've read in the newspapers? If so, who are my characters and how is this going to affect them? Some good fiction has been written by writers trying to get at the truth behind the headlines. They imagine themselves as thieves, runaways, murderers, victims in some of the bizarre events reported daily. There are political movements, social trends; possibilities are endless.

   c. In a group of friends or in a family?

   d. Between two people? If so, who are they? What do they want? What do they have at stake?

4. Do I want to begin with a confrontation? If so, ask: Who are these

people and what do they want? What do they have at stake? Do I want to write about:

    a. Meeting?
    b. Parting?
    c. An admission of guilt and recrimination? Reconciliation?
    d. Attack?
    e. Pursuit and flight?
    f. Betrayal?
    g. Courtship or breakup?
    h. Intrusion?
    i. A business meeting?
    Or do I want to write about a completely different kind of confrontation?

Remember, these are only a few of an unlimited number of starting places. Your own possibilities are expanded by your knowledge of who you are, where you came from and what internal and external forces drive you. If, however, you've reached the bottom of this checklist without any clear idea of what you want to do, you may want to begin with an exercise.

1. Somebody is running. You become that person. What are you running from and why?
2. Write about somebody packing for a trip. Who? What is going into the suitcase? Where is the person going and why?
3. Write about an accident.
4. Write about a loss.
5. Somebody forgets something important. What happens?
6. Write about somebody in a doctor's office.
7. A child is crying on the doorstep. Become the child. A stranger approaches. Become the stranger.
8. You are behind a car in which a struggle is going on.
9. A telegram has just arrived.
10. You are trying to place an urgent telephone call.

If these exercises seem too specific for you, try making up a few of your own, or sitting down with a notebook and making lists of possibilities until you arrive at your own point of departure.

What to Remember

Now comes the hard part, which is as wonderful and exciting as it is daunting. It's time to sit down and begin. As you do, there are some things it helps to remember.

    1. Nothing you write is wasted. I learned this from my first agent, who was

turning down yet another of my early stories; she was right. The busted story turned out to be instead a rough sketch for my first novel.

   2. Nothing you write is carved in stone. You want to feel comfortable with your work, even proud of it, but you need to stay flexible. Be prepared to rewrite when and where necessary because:

   a. *You want to do whatever you need to, to make your work as good as you can make it.*

   b. *You're finding out what you have to say as you forge the words to say it.* More about this later.

   3. Writing is learned on the job, and the only real teacher is experience. And most important:

   4. Writing, you are discovering your material. Defining and selecting your options, you're on your way to developing the inner logic that will direct your story. Writing, you're finding out what you have to write about.

   Writing is the only way you can find out what you have to write about. Reading may show you the way, but you won't know for sure what you have to say or how to say it until you have begun writing.

2

DEVELOPMENT

efore you have decided what to write about, the number of options is daunting. You can write about anything in the world — that is, *anything you can think of*. The limitations are already established because that is *you* making the choices. Once you have decided what to write about, the options narrow further because you have discarded the rest of the possibilities to concentrate on this one. As you work, each choice along the way opens a new avenue of choices, and each of these choices is individual because you are an individual.

The science fiction writer Brian Aldiss reported seeing a Czech cartoon at a film festival. At each step the audience was invited to choose one of four options for the cartoon characters. If Fuzzy fell into the manhole, was he going to: A. Climb back out; B. Bounce back out; C. Rise majestically on a waterspout from a broken pipe; or, D. Start on a journey through the sewers? Each audience choice channeled the story into a new set of four choices designed for that particular story line, but the masterminds who planned the cartoon had to come up with possible story lines for every choice among each set of options at every step along the way and the number of potential stories they had to develop increased geometrically so that the total was astronomical.

Writing, you are dealing with more choices than the Czech cartoonists could develop with the aid of a computer and several animation studios working day and night for a hundred years. The crucial difference is that your own range of choices is informed by the composition of your own alluvial sludge, by your inclinations and circumstances and dozens of other factors unique to you, down to what you think you are doing, which is often only the visible part of what you are actually doing.

Until you actually begin putting down words to tell the story, your choices are determined by who you are. From the moment the first sentence casts itself, there is another factor: the inner logic of that particular story, which is going to determine your choices *within the framework of that particular story.* This is the set of rules a story makes for itself as it goes along. It determines what can and ultimately will happen within a particular fictional framework.

I believe a good short story creates its own inevitability. Even when the work comes quickly you are making dozens of conscious choices and discarding hundreds of others, and as you make these choices the inner logic determines them, precluding anything that does not of its nature belong. It will determine style and diction even as style and diction help define the inner logic of this particular story; it will determine what the characters can and can't do, what they sound like and what they look like, what is going to happen and, in the end, the shape the story assumes.

Inner Logic

The inner logic of a story begins casting itself with the first sentence. As you begin to write, you will see how each choice you make determines your options farther down the line. With the first sentence you are beginning to establish who the central character is, what are the prose rhythms, where you as author are going to stand and where as observer/actor your central character is going to stand. Whether tragic or comic, you are setting the tone.

Beginning a story, look at your first paragraph and try to decide who these people you're inventing are and what they're doing here. You may need to work out the answers to these questions on the job — as you're developing your options and then narrowing them, but from the outset you can ask:

1. What is my story about? Am I writing about small or large changes in a sensitive emotional situation or is this going to be a story about action or suspense? A mystery? Something else? If so, what?

2. Am I standing off from my characters or working from close in? A third-person narrator who sees everything and everybody from the outside is going to create one kind of story; an emotional first-person narrator with an urgent need to tell everybody how what happened to her happened, creates quite another.

3. Do the narrative choices I've made so far make my intentions clear or do they get in the way? Consider tone of voice. Point of view. Character names. For instance: if you think you're writing a sensitive romance, a character named Howdy Sue Clampett is going to give readers a different idea.

4. Does the language I'm using help or hurt? We'll talk about style at greater length later. For the moment, a simple example: overblown, flowery prose is likely to pull all the teeth out of an action story.

5. Am I more interested in what's going on inside my characters' heads or what's happening to them as a result of external factors — fire, flood or social change?

6. Am I trying to be funny or tragic or both?

Beginning to write a story, you may not know the answers to many of these questions, but the answers start to develop *from the first paragraph* because you are being forced to make narrative decisions. If you're not ready to apply these hard questions to your own work, pick up a short story collection — any "best" anthology will do — and read the *first paragraphs* of several of the stories, applying the list of questions above. Then go on to read the rest of each story. You'll find you already know a great deal more than you thought about each one because *from the first paragraph* the authors were hard at work making their intentions clear.

Let me show you how this can work.

Discovering Narrative Options

Here is an opening I have made up to give you an idea of how a story can make itself. A child is telling us about his grandmother's house:

My grandmother's house was bigger than anyplace I ever lived with my mother and father. Our houses got smaller while hers didn't seem to have any end to it. Her place was filled with furniture that always looked like it was leaning forward, crouching, and if you turned your back on it, it was going to fall on you. I used to tiptoe in the middle of the hall with my elbows in tight against my sides because I was afraid I was going to jiggle the big glass-fronted bookcases and they would fall, and if the falling furniture didn't kill me my grandmother would hear the noise and come to the kitchen door, scolding me for ruining everything.

We already know this is the child telling the story. His diction indicates that he is still a child with fresh and painful memories of something that happened recently. We also know that we are going to see things as he sees them and know only what he tells us, although he may tell us more than he realizes.

There are already so many things going on in this first paragraph that it would be possible to extract a dozen stories. I'll go after one, exploring the options.

What is the child doing at the grandmother's? Is it an afternoon visit or has he been left there while the parents are away? It's possible that he is trapped in his grandmother's house forever; he has to live there because the parents are dead. Instead let's say they're only away. Where have they gone, and why? Maybe they are in New York for the weekend, or maybe they have gone to help a friend in trouble or to try to save a brother or sister (another child of that same grandmother) who is sick, or dying, or depressed. If the parents are away, how much does the child know about the real reasons? The decision affects the story; it's already obvious that there is a potential story.

Let's say the parents are divorcing; they have gone to the city to see lawyers. The child may suspect because he has heard little things but doesn't really want to put the pieces together. It is important to him to pretend not to know. Does he know more than the grandmother or does she know and the child not know? Let's say the grandmother knows and the child doesn't know, or thinks he doesn't.

What is the relationship between child and grandmother? He's been shrinking in hallways, afraid of making her mad, so he must be a little afraid of her. He says he's afraid of the furniture, but that isn't what he means. He is a little afraid of her. We now know that he is uncomfortable with this grandmother, depressed by her house and upset by his parents' unhappiness, which he must sense even though he pretends not to know about it.

Here is this unhappy child tiptoeing through the halls with the old lady in the kitchen (she seems forbidding but she is probably a wonderful cook) and he is miserable, which she may or may not guess. She may be too depressed by the parents' breakup to pay any attention to him. He is also worried about all that furniture, and it seems logical that what happens to him will have something to do with the furniture.

Probably he is going to break something, which is bound to precipitate a scene with the grandmother. It may seem like an accident but he has probably brought it on because he has to do something to change his circumstances; consciously or unconsciously, he has to trigger a scene with the grandmother because otherwise he will just keep on walking down those halls being afraid of that furniture and there won't be any story.

Since he has already told us about the glass-fronted bookcases it is likely that whatever happens will involve them. Maybe he will start to climb one, to reach a certain book, and the thing will topple and fall on him. In a less melodramatic vein maybe he will try and climb the hatstand and it will fall and break the glass in one of the bookcases; whatever happens, it is the furniture that suffers, not the boy, but the noise will bring the grandmother into the hall to confront him.

Within this framework, the scene which ensues has already defined itself to some extent.

1. It is likely that the grandmother is not as stern as she seems for the simple reason that no living human exists in only one dimension. A beginning writer dealing with any human is like a would-be musician sitting down at a chord organ; the possibilities are extraordinary. Then: if the grandmother is stern, she is probably disturbed by the impending divorce, by the fact that she has to take care of this child without letting him know why she is disturbed or that she is disturbed because the parents won't want him to know anything about it until everything is settled.

2. She may resent his presence because he is the emblem of her unhappiness. There are dozens of possible ways for this to work itself out. Here are the most likely ones.

a. The child's mother is her daughter. If this is the case, she probably connects the boy with the father and blames him because the father isn't here to blame. Eventually she is going to understand that they are not the same person, that this child's needs are deep and real and she has to set aside the absent father and deal directly with the child.

b. Or his father is her son. If this is the case, she looks at him and sees her own son in him. She sees him as boy and as man, sees all the past promise and present misery, and because she is trying to distance pain she has kept the child at arm's length.

I like the second premise; she is the *father's* mother, and in the scene which begins, theoretically, because of the broken bookcase, the child's fears and her fears for him all emerge. He is crying; she puts her arms around him. Helping him, she takes comfort from him and from the fact that she can help him. He understands that although she seems to be angry about the furniture there is something much worse bothering her, something he is going to have to admit to himself now. So the two are thrown together in mutual sorrow and comfort, closer than they have ever been.

She'll probably say she has always hated those bookcases and take him off to the kitchen, where she will involve him in helping her make cookies or prepare supper: some project that will make them both feel better.

This is only one of the thousand ways a story can build itself.

I believe fiction casts itself in the first sentence. The problem is being willing to cast and recast that first sentence until it is *right* and what follows becomes inevitable. Sometimes a writer can see a story whole, from the beginning; at other times it reveals itself only in the process. It may emerge successfully — a living entity — or it may drop dead before the last page rolls out of the typewriter. The only way to find out is to try and develop an idea of your own, choosing, sifting, discarding, refining.

I made up all that about the grandmother as I went along. Even though I will never write a story from this beginning, even though I made it all up to make a few points about possibilities and development, the paragraph has its own authority. It says what it can and can't do.

The story line as I developed it is implicit in the opening lines. The diction tells us that this is the child speaking and he is still in childhood. We sense his mood, which is elegiac. We already know something about his feelings for the house, for the grandmother, and we have some sense of his uneasiness at the time. We know he is telling about something he remembers, that the story belongs to him, and we will see everything through his eyes. Each of the options I developed for this story had within it a certain number of possibilities, but each progressive possibility was determined by what already existed. In developing the story, I could not violate what went before. If Uncle Harry walked in and picked up the boy and took him off to Tulsa, that would violate the story. If the grandmother murdered the child and stuffed him in the clothes drier, that would violate the story. If the parents came back and took him home before he resolved the tension between himself and the house and the grandmother, that would violate the story.

What I've set up—a closed circumstance in which the boy and his grandmother are alone in the house, with nobody expected—a human story about ordinary people (no hatchet murderers implied or expected) dictates a solution to the story in human terms, in an everyday way—close interaction between two closely related people put in conflict.

Because the story made its own rules, the options broadened to a certain point and then began to narrow as I homed in on the resolution. Most writers find beginnings difficult precisely because they mean dealing with that multitude of options. As they go along, these same writers usually gather momentum, finishing a work of fiction with certainty because at a certain point the options do begin to narrow. This narrowing of options determines the ending. Because that was me and not you making the decisions at every point about the boy and his grandmother, and because the story was growing along lines that made themselves clear as I made the choices, it had to end the way it did.

If this sounds arbitrary, let it. Trying to understand writing fiction without writing is like trying to learn to swim by sitting on the edge of the pool and listening attentively to the instructor. Unless you get wet, you know nothing. If you have already written a few stories you will be able to see how the options establish themselves. Writing more stories, you will learn to recognize the point at which the options narrow, in short, how a story develops and how it creates its own inevitability. Look at the example I have given you, of the boy and his grandmother.

Now look at the first paragraph of your own story and ask yourself:

1. Who is the central character here? What kind of person? How is this person defined or limited by who he/she is? By external circumstances? The little boy and the grandmother in my example are limited by their relative ages and by what they know and don't know. Yours have equal limitations.

2. How are my characters defined or limited by setting? In my example, boy and grandmother are essentially limited to the house. Whether yours are on a ranch or at sea or in a one-room apartment or in a big city, setting is going to have some effect on them. Studying your setting, see how it makes rules for them.

3. How are my characters defined or limited by situation? The boy and his grandmother have been thrown together because there's trouble in the family. See what effect the situation you have in mind is going to have on your characters.

4. How are my characters defined or limited by what they know or don't know? Boy and grandmother are set in opposition because she knows what's going on with the parents but he can only guess. Decide what your characters know or don't know about what's going on and you'll begin to develop a pretty good idea of what they're going to do and how they'll respond.

5. What do my characters *want*? At bottom, both boy and grandmother want to be loved and understood, but because of the circumstances, they're going to have to work hard to reach this point. Knowing what your own characters *want*, ask yourself:

a. Do they want the same things?

b. Do they each want something different?

c. How is this going to make them behave?

6. How are my characters defined or limited by the way they feel about each other? Boy and grandmother are uncomfortable with each other, wary, afraid of what's going on with the boy's parents. You're entering the territory of *action* and *reaction*. Knowing what you already do about them from the answers to the first five questions, set your characters in motion and you'll begin to know how they're going to behave in the circumstances you create for them. This is what determines how your story works.

If you have trouble answering these questions about your own work, it's probably time to go back to your story and take a second look. Ask yourself:

What do I need to change here to discover the answers, or to make them clear to readers?

Remember, I've already suggested that *Nothing you write is carved in stone.* And: *Writing, you find out what you have to write.*

Now for the rest of the package. I believe *you find out what you have to say in the process of working out the way you're going to say it.*

The most important thing I have to tell you and the hardest to learn is how important it is to be willing to take a second look.

3

Rewriting to Complete Your Thinking

*F*irst stories, even by gifted writers, are likely to be short, sketchy at best. *This is because you as beginning writer have not learned to complete your thinking.*

Scenes may be hinted at or briefly described instead of dramatized. The big moments are often underplayed or completely lost. Revising, *you as writer will learn how to get the most out of the work you've already done by completing your thinking.*

You are *learning how to develop your material.*

By development, I mean using everything that comes to hand — all your talent and hard work — to make your story as complete as it needs to be, and as good as you can make it. You're finding out what you have to say in the process of working out the best way to say it. This means everything from choosing the specific word — for instance Bengal tiger instead of animal, or amble, shamble, stride, glide or stumble instead of *walk* — to sharpen the impression you're giving your reader, to learning what to put in and what to leave out to enhance your material.

Hard as the need to rewrite is to come to terms with, especially for beginners, it's an essential part of this complex and rewarding process. Looking at your initial narrative decisions, you test each one, from word choices to what to put in and what to leave out, asking yourself — is this working for me or is it working against me? Then you refine and focus through revision.

If you can learn to do this *from the first minute you sit down to write*, you'll discover that you know more about it than you thought you did: Who the people are, what they want, where the story is going.

As you write and rewrite, your story develops on several levels. You're judging your initial choices and adding, changing and altering as you get a clearer idea of what you want to accomplish. Some writers like to bash out a quick first draft and then go back to make refinements, but I prefer to get the first sentence *right* before going on to the second, the first paragraph *right* before going on, and so on. Either way:

1. You're finding your story and pulling up the right details so you can make your reader see what you see. You'll be sharpening the *focus*.

2. Working on the way you express yourself, finding the right words to tell *this particular story*, telling it *as best you can*, you're refining your material and trying to get the best out of it.

3. Rethinking, you're going deeper into what drives your characters, exploring their reasons for doing what they're doing and their feelings about them so you can make this clear to the reader. The story won't necessarily get longer, but it will get *denser*, tighter, more clearly directed to your point.

4. Examining the order of events, questioning yourself at each point about what's going on and whether it belongs (remember the process of exploring options), *you're completing your thinking and making a stronger story.*

Try to stay flexible and get comfortable with the idea of revision *from the minute you begin your story*, and you'll find it easier.

Like so many things about writing fiction, this can only be learned *on the job.* To find out what you have to say, you need to make a beginning.

Remember it is only a beginning. Nothing you write is carved in stone and almost everything you write will benefit from rewriting. I should say at the outset that if any of you are going to make it in show biz, that is, if any of you are going to write fiction that pleases anybody besides yourself and possibly your most doting relative, you are going to have to develop the habit of rewriting. I was twenty-five years old before I learned this and I had to learn it the hard way, with my trunk already lined with crippled and blighted short stories. If I don't give you anything else, I would like to help you make the shortcut to this inevitable discovery.

Admit the hard fact. Use it. Nothing you write is ever perfect the first time around. As you mature as a writer you will understand this from the inside, watching your work grow under your hands and improve with each revision. First choices are not always the best choices; you as writer do not always know how to give the reader what you know and take as a given. Rewriting helps the writer bridge the gap between intention and execution but there is more to the process than the simple perfection of manner. Just because you have made a stab at telling a story, and gotten some of it down, does not mean that you have gotten it all, or in the best way, or that you have developed a sketch into a living story or even guessed at the subtleties. Process helps the story to develop.

At the risk of starting a fist fight, I am ready to say that a great deal emerges in the forging of the language, that stories do indeed develop in the process, and that you as writer have to be willing to write and rewrite what you've already done in order to bring it in line with what you think you're doing. The function of all this rewriting, which is, in fact, recasting, is to enable you to run at the wall again and again until you are up and over. You find out what you think in the process of finding out the best way to say it.

We have a Pulitzer Prize-winning friend, a novelist of considerable stature, who showed us a new novel some years ago. My resident critic had the colossal nerve to say something he has said to me more than once: "I like it, but I think it needs to go once more through the typewriter."

Because this was a *real* writer with a long career, he did not stalk away in a huff. Instead he thanked us both and went away to put the novel once more through the typewriter. Several years and seven versions later, he had fulfilled his original intentions in a beautiful work of great power.

Although there are occasional visitations, or gifts — short stories or chapters that present themselves to the writer, whole, with no need for revision — most fiction comes more slowly. Like a photograph, a story takes time to develop. If you lift it out too fast, and call it finished, you may end up with nothing more than a pale suggestion of what might have been.

If you are a draft writer, and can bring yourself to do it, you may gain from putting away your first draft for a few days or weeks, with the idea of returning to it later. It may attract additional notes like lint, but even if it doesn't, you will be surprised when you take it out again. You will discover that you have work to do. You will see just where the execution falls short of your intention, where you can clarify or amplify. Nuances and added values will present themselves. What you want to make clear will become clearer.

A writer who works sentence by sentence, paragraph by paragraph, discovers the same thing. If you are the kind who needs to rework the first sentence, the first paragraph, the first page, before you go on to the next, you will discover that by the time you reach the second page, it is already partially developed; it was developing in your mind as you worked out the first sentences.

Between the first and second drafts of a story, or even of a sentence, you are learning about what you are doing: what belongs and what doesn't, what you forgot to put in the first time around, which were your false steps and what you need to do to bring to the page the shape you have in mind.

If you read and reread your cherished prose and still can't bear to change a word, sit down and begin the simple mechanical business of copying it over, whether you are writing by hand or keyboard.

Once more through the typewriter.

Even if the changes are slight, the work is going to change under your hands. It's going to grow. It will develop as you complete your thinking.

You'll see.

This kind of reworking is not simply a matter of making the work better technically. You are involved in getting at what you really have to write about, and the ways in which you will write about it.

Your librarian can point you to published facsimiles of manuscripts by famous writers, various drafts with all their crossings-out and inclusions. *Revision*, (Writer's Digest Books) is filled with examples from manuscripts of real works in progress by published writers. In almost every case a careful reader can look at the authors' changes to get an idea of how the process of revision helped them to complete their thinking, but you will learn about this best through you own writing, rewriting, re-rewriting to get at the truth of what you have to say and to find the best way to say it.

For the moment let's work with a simple example, cobbled on the spot to illustrate. Here are some versions of a first sentence:

1. The road to Cecily's house was long and hard.
2. He found the road to Cecily's house harder than he expected.

This second version slides into point of view; here's a man who's going along a road that's hard for him. The next choice pops up. Is it hard because it's rocky or steep, or because there's something going on that he's finding hard to accept?

3. Although it was a perfectly ordinary road, winding through perfectly ordinary suburbs, David found the road to Cecily's house harder than he expected. Of course these things were never easy.

Notice that the character has picked up a name and we've gotten a first glimpse of the landscape. But a number of other elements have crept in. For instance: "These things were never easy." Hey, wait. What things? David seems to be on an unpleasant errand. Recasting, I've slipped from refining the prose into expansion and development.

4. Although it was a perfectly ordinary road, winding through perfectly ordinary suburbs, David found the road to Cecily's house harder than he expected. Of course these things were never easy. At the moment he couldn't be certain which would be harder — telling her he was going to prison or that he's stopped being in love with her.

Even though this is only an example, there is a story implicit in this rough first paragraph.

You need to move inside your own story and find out firsthand where your story is and how it's going to develop. Moving inside a story as writer is like going to a different country with its own particular language and its own inhabitants and its own rules about what can and can't be done there.

The only way you can find out what the rules of this particular country are is by testing them. You may even break a few.

Acknowledge it and be willing to try again. Again. As many times as it takes to move into your story, bag and baggage, and make yourself at home there.

As you work you are engaged in a process of selection and rejection which will make your work yours alone. It began when you decided what you wanted to write about. It continues as you choose ways to convey it: language, vantage point, characters — there are hundreds of choices. It intensifies as you try to select the right words to make what you want to make. If you care enough about it, and push yourself hard enough, you can make that story fulfill itself in such a way that it could not have been written by anybody else. You are putting your own stamp on your own material.

It is this business of distillation, of choosing and discarding, transforming the mass of raw experience and forging words to express it, which establishes the inner logic of a piece of fiction. This is more than a matter of technical mastery. It embraces and defines the relationship between you and your work: why you write, what you are trying to do. It will determine the final shape of the story and at the same time help you achieve it. Writing and rewriting, you will begin to develop a sense of *what is right for a particular story*, what belongs and what doesn't belong, how to get where you are going. As you get better at what you are doing, you will see how this works. You will make fewer wrong choices and find it easier to rework when necessary. You will discover that it is more productive to explore better ways of doing what you set out to do than it is to waste energy defending your first choices. What you have to say — your preoccupations, your central material — will emerge as you write and rewrite in the process of finding the best way to say it. I think this inner logic determines — may even be — that which the critics so love to pursue and try to capture and dissect: they call it form. Inner logic isn't going to present itself all at once. It isn't even going to present itself every time. It will not present itself at all unless you are willing to engage in the process. Unless you are willing to write and rewrite and rewrite again you will never find out who you are, as writer, or what you have to say.

A student once asked me why I put so much stress on writing in quantity during the course of a term: writing and more writing and rewriting. My answer stands. You're going to have to write a lot of crap in your life before you write anything good, so you might as well get started.

Writing and rewriting, you discover what you have to say.

4

CHARACTER

ome writers like to stand outside a story and make decisions: I'll put in one of these and two of these and a couple of those. I do not believe this is the way the best fiction makes itself. As writer, I need to discover my fiction from the inside, moving inside my characters for as long as the story is happening, letting them move out to create the story. Who are these people, what is the matter with them? What has brought them to this moment? More important, what do they *want*? It is this compulsion, this *wanting* that moves characters as diverse as Herman Melville's Captain Ahab and J.D. Salinger's Holden Caulfield, and draws us as readers along with them, moving us wherever the authors want to take us.

Once you as writer know what your characters *want*, you will know what they are going to do, what they will and won't say — what will happen to them. If there is such a thing as plot, my own characters make it, with their peculiarities and their desires. If one wants one thing and another wants another, then tension exists; the action will follow from this tension. There is only one way for you to discover what your characters *want*, and that is to become them. You will move inside their heads bag and baggage, look through their eyes and think in their cadences. In addition to bringing your own experience to a fictional situation, as does a Method actor, you will go the actor one better. The actor is becoming one character, working with other actors who will become the other characters. Peopling a story, you will to some extent become all the characters.

Moving into character is easier than you think. You are writing firsthand about a state you know, the human state, which is, inevitably, easier than writing about the animal state or a Balkan state — someplace you've never been. We all got into the people business on the ground floor, and whether or not you are comfortable in the company uniform, you know about this from the inside. If you are this person, you can become the people in the stories this person writes.

What's more, you have been writing character for years. Think. The same impulse that inclines you toward excuses and gossip and speech writing and bouts of paranoia informs every character you will ever be.

We all begin writing character sometime in early childhood:

Mom is going to kill me when she finds out I spilled the black paint all down the front door, she's going to say, I told you a hundred times not to touch that paint, and even if I tell her it was an accident, I was trying to make the stupid front door nice for Daddy, she's going to spank me anyway.

This is simple projection, based on what we know about Mom from living with her: that she hates messes and spanks when she gets mad, but we have given her lines to say and assumed actions for her when she isn't even on the scene.

Schoolyard gossip is another form of projection: "Well she said she got that sweater from her rich uncle but you know what a liar she is, I said, I never saw any rich uncle, and she got all embarrassed and said, You never get to see him because he only visits on weekends. Well if you want to know what I think, I think she stole that sweater because I saw one just exactly like it in Schine's Department Store, and I bet she's down there at this very minute, stealing socks to match." The girl talking doesn't have the foggiest idea where that other girl is, but she is projecting from traits already observed and surmised, drawing from her awareness of her own less admirable instincts. Using her inside knowledge of peoplehood, she is writing character.

Adult gossip at its best, which is to say at its most entertaining and least judgmental or damaging, is a more sophisticated version of this. We swap bits of information and then, using the sum of known information, leap into surmise, weaving tales to entertain ourselves on long winter evenings. Because the amount of what's known is small compared to what is not known — other people's motives — we are engaged in writing character: projecting on what we know about these people to draw stories about what we think led them to a certain moment: the divorce, the public insult or the comic extravaganza. Drawing on what we see, we make up whole lives for these people — lives we couldn't possibly see. What we are doing is, at one level, attempting to understand, and at another, attempting to shape or control some part of the mysterious and amorphous, often terrifying business of life. We are already telling stories.

Another manifestation of this gift for writing character is speech writing. We all do it, and it becomes more elaborate as we get older. All of us have enormous collections of great undelivered speeches: the witty last word, the unspoken riposte. The first is written some time in early childhood, when the mean kid down the block does something vicious and then leaves before we can think of anything scorching to say. Or else the teacher blames us unjustly and there is no way to explain, or a parent drives one of us to rage and respect demands our silence. The victim will write dozens of undelivered speeches.

Mine number in the thousands, and some of them are recent. I can remember unrealized dialogs with mean little girls and teachers and parents in which I emerged the victor, witty and devastating because I am the unacknowledged master at writing the unspoken last word, whether in answer to the person who is trying to sell funeral plots over the telephone or to the snake at the cocktail party who likes to come up with the concealed stiletto and slip it between the ribs.

The other side of the coin is wish fulfillment: speeches in which I accept recognition, laurels, fame with a gracefully bowed head. From grammar school on, I wrote delightful dialogs with the cute boy in the third row, in which I found out he liked horses too, or we stumbled on a common love of reading in the children's division of the public library.

The salient point here is that great undelivered speeches are almost always accompanied by great unspoken answers.

"Madam, that's the fourth time you've broken into this line. The rest of us have groceries too."

"Oh dear, how stupid of me. Please accept my apologies."

Or, on a more elevated level:

"You've been badmouthing me for eighteen years, Dad, all you can see is a dumb kid that never gets an A, well I want you to read this novel I'm writing, then you'll see."

"Herbie, it's brilliant, how could I have been so blind?"

Since the other person is absent, the writer can make up lines for himself and the other person without ever being challenged. Writing lines for other people, we are assuming character.

I'm convinced that this chronic writing of parts for other people is common to most of us. In some of us, it takes over. I haven't done any more than a cocktail-party survey, but I can report that all the writers I know construct scenes at the drop of a hat partly for fun and partly because they can't help it.

A: "What if we get there and Marlene won't stop talking? I mean, that woman starts talking the minute a warm body passes close enough to her sensors, it doesn't matter who, she just keeps talking until you move away." (*This is an exaggeration of observed qualities.*)

B: (*Carrying it one step farther just for fun.*) "We could take the dog and let her talk to him. He's big and warm and if you squint your eyes he almost looks like a person. She's nearsighted anyway."

A: (*Inventing.*) "What if there's a quiz at the end?"

B: "We'll just wing it."

A: "No, dummy, *if you flunk she'll tell you the whole thing all over again.*"

B: "I know what. The minute she starts, I'll fall out of my chair."

A: "And I'll have to take you to the emergency room."

B: "Right, I'll fall out of my chair and you'll have to take me to the emergency room."

A: "Yeah, but what if she comes along in the ambulance?"

Inventing, that pair can go on all night. Although this scene-writing ability exists in everybody, writers seem to be preternaturally caught up in it, which accounts for the prevalence of that other phenomenon which contributes to our innate sense of character and, incidentally, our habit of fiction. It is implicit in the scene invented above: inventor as victim, or, more simply, paranoia.

As a child I spent a certain amount of time waiting in the car while my mother was inside the store, and I never quite shook the idea that one of those days she was not coming out. What would I do? Waiting in the car I wrote scenes in which the police came and found me, I wrote scenes with my remaining relatives, scenes at the orphanage, the scene titled The Funeral. I even wrote scenes in which the cute boy in the third row took me home to his mother and father ("Oh, you poor thing," the parents would say, already loving. There would be a fireplace glowing at their backs and my favorite dinner would be cooking. The cute boy would be waiting to help me with my homework and they would all say, "We'll take care of you.")

I wrote dozens of other scenes out of other fears: THEY would bomb St. Petersburg, Florida, and when that happened the enemy would do X and I would do Y. Or I really had appendicitis or bubonic plague, and the following things were going to happen, beginning with the discovery of the distended abdomen or those telltale nodules in the armpits. My assumptions about my actions were perfectly natural; after all, I thought I knew what I would do in a given set of circumstances, and I began to believe I knew what other people would do. In writing these scenes out of assorted fears I was, again, assuming character for others.

Writing from character should be easy because, to some extent, everybody does it. A would-be psychologist has given me a textbook term for this particular habit, as it applies to writers: A.R.T. The initials stand for accuracy of role-taking; it makes sense. Most writers do it at the typewriter and away from it, to the distraction of friends and relatives and the occasional astonishment of somebody who can't figure out how the writer *knew*. At our desks we may begin making terrible faces, assuming gestures, getting up to try a particular stance; some people even discover themselves playing entire scenes, moving from one place to another so they can do all the voices. We learn to be everybody all at once.

If this is not already a habit with you, it's worth trying.

1. Become a member of your immediate family. How does it feel to be inside that body? How does it change the way you feel about yourself? The way you move?

2. You are your least favorite teacher. It's the end of a long day. What are you looking forward to? What's the first thing you're going to do when you get home?

3. You're old. You've been waiting all day for somebody who hasn't come. Now it's dark. What are you going to do?

Moving Into Character

At a certain point, earlier on than you might want to admit, this ceases to be an intellectual operation. As a high school student on an interminable ride from Washington, D.C., to Florida, I saw two kids fighting in the sandy dirt next to a Georgia road. In the next second I *was* one of them, felt the back of my head cracking against the hard, dry dirt, felt the weight of the other kid on top of me, his hands on my shoulders, lifting me so he could throw me down again. I could go on to tell you everything about that life I never lived because it was my life for that fraction of a minute. To try to explain further would be to walk all over the mystery. It happens. It will happen to you, if you let it.

You can write character because you become all your characters. You can be man or woman because they are people before they are men or women; there are so many common traits and hopes and responses that, male or female, people have, with the single incredible biological exception, all those human traits in common. Writers are hundreds of people and they are all real because no matter how different they may be from one another, they are all the writer.

Add to this faculty your storehouse of knowledge. You have already accumulated a complete wardrobe for any possible occasion; you can assume any of the costumes you have seen in your life or combine some of the elements to invent new ones. The same is true of gestures: the ways certain people respond when they are angry or anxious or affectionate; the ways in which they express themselves, from small details of body language to entire speeches. You will not look at some friend or relative and try to draw him exactly as he stands in the particular pair of shoes you last saw him wearing. Instead, you will take as your own certain mannerisms, little bits of his history, observed or imagined attitudes, actions or kinds of reaction, assimilating them so that when you reach into your storehouse to draw on them, you will use them as your own.

Because as writers we are engaged in making something out of something, we take what we have learned from this kind of observation and add it to the different kinds of firsthand experience I have listed. We will take both as necessary equipment when we move inside a character. Instead of thinking: What would I do if I were this person and these things happened to me, you will become that person and you'll know. The writer moves inside the character rather like a Japanese puppeteer, more or less invisible but present nonetheless. When this character talks, his speech begins inside the writer's ear. Each character has his own cadences, his own specific vantage point. He has a certain relationship to other people in the story and certain attitudes toward them. These will all control his speech and actions at the same time as they emerge from them.

Once you have moved inside your character, you will move out together to make the story.

It all happens very fast.

For example:

An old man shambles onto the scene, saying, "Ah been in this town, man and boy, for sixty years now, and I never seen the likes of Bessie Sue."

We already know something about him from the outside. He was shambling when we saw him, so he is either ailing or relaxed or both. From his tone we know he is either uneducated or consciously fixed on country diction, which will inform his speech and his way of looking at things. He is apparently proud of his place in the town and he is both interested in other people and, depending on what we find out about Bessie Sue, either easily surprised or hard to surprise. He likes reminiscence and, from his tone, he seems to like telling stories. He may go on to say, with gentle regret, "Everybody loved her from the first," adding, "for a while, even I was in love with her." The minute he does, new doors fly open.

Moving inside, we will see Bessie Sue through his eyes, we will know how he loved her and how he feels about her now. We'll probably find out *through his memory of it* what they were both like when they were young, what she has done just now to bring her back to his attention. Maybe she's coming back to town and they are going to meet again after all these years. It seems logical to assume the story is going to be about their meeting: his feeling about it ahead of time, how she's changed, what they will do.

Or:

An ordinary man comes home to find his wife crouched in the corner of the kitchen, huddled in a blanket. Her hair looks like a bird's nest, her skin is so pale it looks transparent and when he tries to find out what's the matter she won't talk to him.

Finding her like that, we are with him, we *are* him, because most of us like to think of ourselves as ordinary at least part of the time. Unfolding the mystery, what brought her to this moment, we have to become her. If this is the result of a compound of housewifely frustration and madness, then we will draw on our own darker side to comprehend and draw that madness. If she was terrorized by an intruder, we will draw on that same dark side — our fears, our worst instincts — to become the kind of person who would do that to a woman. Although most of us don't know much about would-be rapists or homicidal maniacs firsthand, or from the inside, we are able to draw on what we do know to project from it, because we have a firsthand knowledge of violence from our own petty rages and we know fear through our own specific fears.

Or:

An insurance office is humming along; men and women and machines, from typewriters to computers, all work more or less mechanically. The door opens with a crash and there is a lanky teenager in a red flannel shirt and overalls with knobby elbows and knees showing through the worn-out parts. He is chewing gum and his face is barely visible through all the hair. He says, "Hi, my uncle died. Would you believe I'm your new president?"

I would prefer not to write a story from this kind of beginning; the situation is externally caused. Because it is based in an outside event—that death—the circumstances seem slightly artificial to me, as does the juxtaposition of characters.

Still, I can make character work for me even here. Writing about the boy president, I can be all those outraged people in the office, from the aging office manager to the bright executive who aspires to the throne. I also know what it's like to be a kid thrust into a situation I can't handle. I can imagine what it would be like to be given power under those circumstances, and I would probably share the kid's delight in upsetting all that grim industry.

Once you discover and become your characters, your story begins to draw itself. If you are true to the characters, they will do only what they would do within the limitations of the story as it builds itself, reinforcing the inner logic. In an almost symbiotic way, they will develop your story for you even as you develop them.

More than one writer has been quoted as saying, "I have control over my work up to a certain point and then the characters take over." I think that's an exaggeration but it's one way of demonstrating and insisting on characters as people; if you are all the characters then you *know* what they will do and will not do; you give them life and their life is the life of the story. If you try to make them do anything out of character because of the exigencies of so-called plot they will resist you, and if you treat them falsely the story itself will fail. If you are true to them, they will be true.

The problem then, if there is a problem, is not how to create character or what to do with people once you invent them, but where to begin and how to give them to the reader.

I usually hear my characters before I see them. The minute they open their mouths I know them, and I seem to know as well what it feels like to be inside that particular consciousness. The next thing I do is find out their names. I have a superstitious faith in the naming of names; once I have heard a character and named him, I know him. To me names are people. We all have specific expectations of Bobs or Bills as opposed Hugos or Maxes or Percivals, and Abigails and Marthas are not the same kind of people as Lindas and Dawns; we think we know what kind of person a George is, and we have our own ideas about Janes.

Last names are important to me, too. Are they WASP or ethnic or bland or none of the above, and how does the last name sound in combination with the first? What are the cadences? There are palpable differences between characters named Ralph Smith and Bob Smith and Stroke Smith and Thistleton Smith. We know something in advance about characters named Stanley Kowalski, Jay Gatsby, a little boy named Piggy, grown men named Benjy and Lennie, as opposed to the Jasons and Georges who must take care of them. Whether a name is comic or dashing or nondescript, it casts its own light on character.

With the naming of names, the writer, who is the character, takes a moment to step outside. What does this person look like, and does it matter? As a writer beginning a story, I need to know how old a character is and how he feels inside his body, but how much I give the reader depends on the story. Perhaps because much good comedy is based on detail, comic characters seem to profit from added detail. Probably because I work from the inside, I think physical characteristics matter only as they affect or define character: somebody who is cross-eyed or has a squint or carries an old injury is partially defined by this. Somebody who is colossally ugly or remarkably beautiful is affected by it; those characteristics which differentiate are important — a police-blotter rundown is not.

Readers need some details, but if a writer gives them too much, they are likely to reject or forget. For some of the same reasons "Superman" on radio was an exciting superhero while "Superman" on television was a funny-looking guy in an ill-fitting union suit and even the movie *Superman* has physical limitations, readers want only a few external details to confine their imaginations: they will take what the writer has given and supply the rest. Reading, they too will become and so help create the characters.

They can supply most wardrobe details too. Costume matters only as it matters to the characters. If an aging female frump turns up in flowered beach pajamas and a flossy hat, something is happening. If a beloved son who we all thought was straight as an arrow comes home wearing lamé basketball shoes and a rhinestone brooch it is worth mentioning because he is trying to tell us something. The broker who sheds his three-piece grey suit and starts sitting around in his pajamas is telling us something. Costume changes are important only as they function in the story. There may be times when we need to know a character is wearing Puccis and Guccis or a selection of $3.98 specials from Bradlee's whisper rack, but for the most part, readers can do as good a job of costuming as the writer. Most of them can supply wardrobes for a group of college students or shoppers or a middle-class family; why not let them?

Stances, attitudes and mannerisms are more telling external details. What is that woman doing while she talks? How does she respond when somebody walks out on one of her speeches? How does this man meet his children, with love or resentment or indifference? Does a character enter a room like a parade, with trumpet fanfare and bass drums thumping, or does he come in timidly, waiting for permission to sit down? How do characters' expressions change as they talk, and what are they doing with their hands? Human beings have such a phenomenal vocabulary of grimaces and tics and twitches that it's possible to convey emotions simply by recording one or two gestures as a character speaks.

Try at least one of these people on for size:

1. The first person you see if you look out the nearest window.
2. The next person who waits on you in a store or a restaurant.
3. The person sitting opposite you on the bus.
4. A member of the opposite sex — somebody your age.
5. A member of the opposite sex — much older.
6. A member of the opposite sex — much younger.

What does it feel like to be inside that body? To be wearing those clothes? Why are you doing whatever you happen to be doing right now, in that new body? What do the clothes feel like? Do the shoes fit or are they tight? Is the shirt or dress new or old, are you embarrassed by it or proud of it? What are your hopes and desires; what do you *want*?

Once you have become a character, the character moves out to make the story. Once you know him from the inside and can see him from the outside, you can hold up as many other mirrors as you like. How do other people in the story see him, and how does he react to them? Is he different with different people? How does he respond to frustration, to gratification, to love, to rage? How do you, as writer, feel about him? Yes you *are* him but do you like or hate what you have become and do you want your readers to share your feelings or not?

At its best, this process of becoming one character, of being all the characters and doing all the voices, is a mad combination of projection and ventriloquy, play acting and observation and selection which defies definition and cannot be separated from all the other parts of the process of making fiction so long as you are engaged in it.

Extraordinary as it is, this process is fundamental, and gives back much more than you as writer bring to it. It establishes the inner logic of the story as surely as the diction and the point of view help you define it. If you know your character in this way, from the inside, he will reinforce his own reality:

no amount of pushing and squeezing will make him fit into a situation where he doesn't belong, and no amount of manipulation will get him to do something he would not naturally do. He has taken on his own reality and he won't betray you; he will help you make your story true. Or she will.

Becoming Your Character

Here is a simple exercise to help you get into character. You can easily do it in your head, or you may be more comfortable sitting down with your notebook or at the typewriter or at the computer. Remember, this is only an exercise. The characters you create and move inside as narrator are going to be as distinct and individual as you are.

For the purposes of demonstration, let's say you've decided to become somebody completely different from yourself. You can begin by changing sex. Feel different? It should give you a fresh perspective.

Now you can complete the change by:

1. Changing age. The two simplest places to go for this are:

a. Childhood. Remember what that felt like? Close your eyes and then open them, pretending to be eight years old. How does the room look to you? The light in it? How do the other people you can see look to you? Remember, you're only eight, which means they look *old*.

b. Old age. You're not there yet, but remembering elderly people you know, from your grandparents to people you've seen on the bus or in the street, you can close your eyes and, opening them again, begin to get an idea of what the world looks like to a very old person in failing health. You know what it feels like to be exhausted. Imagine feeling that way all the time. If you've ever sprained an ankle or broken a bone, you can imagine the pain in the joints. Think about having to run across the street at that age. Then, thinking about all the things you remember at your age, whether it's 20 or 70, try to think about the kind and number of memories you'd have in extreme old age.

2. Change your name. What is your new name? Think hard, because it's going to help define you; if it's a nickname, there's information about you in the way you earned it. If it's an ethnic name, certain things are suggested by who your forebears were, and which country they came from. Try on your name. Get comfortable with it.

3. Next, imagine what you look like. Decide what you have on, and what it feels like to be wearing these things.

a. If you're little, you're probably wearing clothes your parents picked out. What do they look like? Do they still fit? Do you like them or hate them? Drawing on memory, decide what you feel like wearing them.

b. If you're the old person, you may be wearing favorite old things or something you hate because you can't afford new clothes. Or you may be dressed to the nines because you have a great stake in what you look like. Ask yourself the same questions about what it's like to be walking around in them.

4. Study the limitations childhood and old age present. As the child, you don't know as much as the grownups; you're running around at the edges of things, trying to figure out what's going on. You probably can't go out without an adult.

As the ancient, fragile person, you may know a great deal about what's going on but you may not be able to do anything about it because you probably can't get around too easily.

    a. What does this do to the way you look at things?

    b. How is it going to affect your behavior?

    c. What are your priorities?

5. Now move into the first person. This character is not *he* or *she* but *I*. You're listening for the tone of voice. Try to imagine what you as child or old person would sound like, both to yourself and to a listener. Start by describing your circumstances in that particular tone of voice; remember that either as child or extremely old person you're limited by your age.

6. Introduce a second person: friend or enemy, parent or child or contemporary in age, lover or villain.

7. Now put them at cross purposes. If you're the old person, committed to comfort and safety, try introducing the child, who wants to disrupt things. What are you, as old person, going to do about this threat to your serenity?

You'll be introducing a factor that puts your character into action. Now get comfortable with that character. Move in and drive around inside that person. If it's a comfortable fit, you'll be able to predict what that person would do in any given circumstance.

Next, choose somebody *you* want to write about, and apply the same set of questions. Once you know the answers, you'll begin to understand what drives that character. And if and as you become that person, with all his or her wants and desires and particular compulsions, you'll have a clear idea how you as character will behave once you move into your story. 📘

5

PLOT, OR: THE LIST
OF THE LUCKY SEVEN

*S*omebody once told me there were only seven basic plots in all fiction. This was probably only a cynic's view, based on overexposure to cheap fiction, but I was little at the time, I was going to grow up to be a writer, and at ten or twelve I still believed all I had to do was collect the necessary information.

I was so taken by the idea of a master list, so nearly convinced that all you needed to write fiction was a dandy plot, that I launched a search for the list of the lucky seven. I would have to confess I was still looking when I finished college. I thought if I could just find it, the list would solve all my problems, even as I used to believe I could write something really terrific if only some kindly grownup would tell me what to *write*.

Maybe there really is a list somewhere, in a time capsule at the top of an isolated mountain, or in a jungle temple surrounded by ferocious native guards, and maybe it is the key to everything, but I never found it and I never met anybody who had seen it firsthand. After I had been writing for a while, I understood that my stories, at least, did not begin with plots but rather developed, sometimes painfully, out of the people I introduced, the way they talked, the sound of the first few sentences and the way they looked on the page. I stopped looking for the list of the lucky seven, and at just about the same time, I ceased to believe in it.

I still believe a perceptive reader can look at a finished story and extract the "plot," as well as gain some sense of the shape and intention, but I think this has to come after the work is finished. Plots taken as starting points are crude things, creaky and predictable, diagrammatic. I think they make for cheap fiction.

I spend a lot of time diagnosing TV patients at the first symptoms and predicting the ends of assorted detective shows in the first five minutes; I can tell you who's going to do what and why, I can usually even tell you when, and I was the first in our row to tumble to the solution to *Murder on the Orient Express*. Perhaps because I grew up on radio soap opera and have cheap tastes in television and still read the funnies, I am familiar with formula. Because I still take a guiltless pleasure in reading the latest schlock bestseller, I can recognize formula from a mile off. Without getting any closer, I can even tell you which one it is. As a result I can predict the ending of almost anything cheap, usually in the first five minutes, right before I fall asleep. I should add that only things I can't figure out ahead of time will keep me awake. Thanks to all those years of mainlining shrinkwrapped narrative courtesy of mass media, I can also sketch neat endings for you on demand. They have very little to do with what I write or the way I write and they have nothing to do with what I spend most of my time reading — the best novels and stories I can find — good fiction from a variety of sources. Perhaps because I am known as Mrs. Plot at our house, I can report that knowing plot, or formula, in that superficial and external way has very little to do with real writing except in a negative way — knowing ahead of time which solutions are hackneyed, tired, cheap.

Beginning writers who talk about plot as a separate entity usually think they have all the necessary equipment — an attractive style, the will to win — and all they need to get going is a good, solid plot. They will tell you in all earnestness that they have some really good characters here, or a wonderful idea, but no plot to go with them, and they're convinced that all they're waiting for is the right rack to hang their words on. They may not know it, or if they know, won't admit that when they say plot they really mean formula. Now formula is necessary and useful to writers engaged in mass-production: *we'll give them the old boy-meets-girl this week, the old star-crossed lovers routine, except this time they'll be in space suits, he's an earthman, see, and her folks are purple because they grew up on this satellite, or else we can do Oedipus in cowboy suits, instead of putting his eyes out he can throw himself in front of the stampede.* It takes some kind of external organization to enable a writer to grind out stories for the pulps or television week after week after week. The writer working according to formula is faced with an easy set of choices and he can make them quickly. He can write easy stories, perhaps even polished ones, but it is possible for him to spend a lifetime on this kind of fiction without ever discovering his central material. If he is doing it for a mass market for pay and he's happy at his work, that's cool, but most writers want more, for some of the same reasons Marilyn Monroe wanted to play Grushenka and almost every stand-up comic dreams of playing *Hamlet*. It's a matter of completeness of expression.

For the writer of serious fiction the idea of writing from formula is pernicious at best, although an accomplished writer can sometimes take an old formula and twist it and make it dance. For the beginner, it can be dangerous.

I think a writer who is serious about making fiction has to be convinced that each decision made about the work is brand new. Although you may in passing take some familiar turnings, discovering some of the same decisions other writers have made, you need to bring them from within yourself after consideration, so that your stamp is on everything you write.

With this in mind, I don't like to talk about plot. When somebody mentions plot as a starting point or treats it as a separate entity to be considered separately, my back hairs rise and I stiffen in my chair.

I prefer to talk about development.

I believe that good stories do have movement, that this is often easy to trace once the story is complete. The writer does not necessarily have to know in advance precisely what this movement is going to be. You may indeed know the story all at once, as you begin or you may instead discover it as you go along. You will sense the movement as your story develops, and if the story has life you're going to discover or arrive at some resolution of this movement as you complete it.

The key is inner logic.

Sometimes a first sentence will appear, whole, and the rest of the story will follow. More often than not beginnings are difficult. Sometimes entire stories are difficult, with the writer grappling with choices at every turn, taking false steps and having to retrace them. At other times the writer will suffer over the initial decisions — who, why, how — only to discover that once they are made the rest is given. If the story has life the writer will progress, sometimes with ease, at other times painfully, from the initial stage of multiple possibilities to the point in the story at which the options begin to narrow, as surely as the shutter of a camera flexes and then snaps to make the picture. This process of development, from the multiplicity of choices to the narrowing of options to make the right ending, is a complex process which cannot be shortcut; most of us have to do a painful lot of bad writing along the way, and nothing, not even a gilt-edged laminated plaque containing the list of the lucky seven plots will help us to escape the hard work involved.

What may help is some external sense of what makes a story, or specific knowledge of certain ways to make a story. There are any number of points of departure, and it may help to try and understand a few of these at the primitive level. Because there is no easy way to talk about all of this and I am a fool for trying, I'm going to make the examples as simple-minded as possible.

I have suggested that for me, at least, stories begin with people. Who are these people and what's the matter with them? What do they *want*?

The more I read and think about fiction and write it, the more certain I am that the best fiction has a strong thread of yearning or desire or compulsion or obsession running through it. The reader is compelled because the characters are compelled in varying degrees, engaged in ways that demand resolution.

Drawn tight, this thread of want creates such tension that the simplest meetings between characters become clashes or collisions. If Jean Valjean was in flight through the pages of *Les Miserables*, there had to be a Javert to chase him. Gatsby yearned for a place in society and Tom Buchanan was there to keep him from it. Philip Roth's narrator in *The Ghost Writer* bundled all his compulsions into the creation and pursuit of a resurrected Anne Frank.

I suspect that people who are completely satisfied with their lot do not become writers. If a fictional character is completely satisfied with his lot and nothing comes along to change this, there isn't going to be any story. For most people, life, at one level or another, is a struggle, and fiction both mirrors and transcends this. Unless you as human being are luckier than all other humans, you are already grappling with hope and despair in varying degrees; fears, wants, both specified and unspecified, needs, ambitions. Recognizing this in yourself, you will find it reflected in your characters.

In addition to knowing who your character is as you step inside, you will begin to understand what this character *wants.* Knowing, you have a way into your story.

Even a partial list of possible characters and the remarkable number of things that might happen to them because of their wants would occupy volumes. Here is one, severely limited.

Take: a farmer. To narrow options at once, let's say he is the white owner of a small farm in the South; he's a recluse. What might he want? Let's eliminate physical objects he might yearn for and ways he might go about trying to get them. Let's say he has no immediate family and is not going to fall in love. What might he want?

1. To be left alone. If this is true you can introduce a visitor from the north, a long-lost relative, an old love, developers of a fast-food stand across the road, new neighbors; any one of a dozen other elements diametrically opposed to his wishes: show him in reaction and have the beginnings of a story which can resolve itself in several ways, up to and including:

    a. His triumph.

    b. His defeat.

    c. His reconciliation.

    d. His refusal to reconcile.

    e. Some other form of change.

2. Or he does not want to be alone. He is lonely. Introduce a visitor, a transient or someone who has come to live with him. If it's a transient you have the beginnings of several stories. Some possibilities include:

    a. The escape of the transient.

    b. The winning over of the transient.

    c. The old man's souring on the idea of company. This raises a new problem: how he tries and whether he succeeds in the matter of driving the transient away. If he fails, is he happy or unhappy? Reconciled or not?

If instead, the person wants to come and live with him, these are some of the possibilities, *among others*:

a. It works out. No story here unless something external happens to threaten the arrangement.

b. In spite of everybody's best efforts, it does not work out. How does the old man get rid of the visitor? Or does the visitor get rid of him?

c. It works so well that they decide to add other people to the arrangement. Others are either willing or unwilling, compatible or not, and the story builds itself around this development. It still stems from the old man's wish for company.

d. It works out but only after the old man has used all his wiles to charm the visitor — or vice versa.

Even this simple example suggests there is no story without *tension* — people and/or things set in opposition with some stake in the outcome.

Development from the wants of characters is inevitable and the progression of possibilities almost geometric. Once a writer moves inside his character and moves out into the story, all that remains is to discover what happens where and when and how. The story is waiting. Making narrative choices, you will narrow the options.

Your people will let you know what they can or can't do. They can only do a limited number of things under the circumstances you have created. If they've been playing serious drama, they're not going to lapse into farce *unless it has been prepared for*; the rapist is not going to repent without reason; the loving mother is not going to commit an ax murder, not unless we've had hints all along that she might not be as sweet as she looks. These characters as you draw them will reach their point of action, or reaction or stupidity or discovery, and they will respond in the only way open to them under the circumstances you have created by moving inside them to discover the story; they command the stage for the climactic moment and then the story is over, because you as writer know what you have set out to discover.

Here are some other ways to begin with people:

1. You can start with X, who is a particular kind of person. What does he love, hate, want, fear, need, and what is he going to do about it? A classic single-character story can bring X into a situation where he gets or doesn't get what he loves or hates, wants or needs or fears, and take him from that point into an infinite number of kinds of discovery. I'll list four possibilities, based on want.

a. He tries like hell and he gets it and is triumphant. A survival story, with emphasis on the ordeal.

b. He gets it and it isn't what he wanted.

c. He doesn't get it and it's just what he wanted.

d. It was just what he wanted and that isn't enough, he wants something more.

How does he react?

2. You can start with X, with his own specific characteristics, and then introduce Y. Who is Y, and what does he want? How do they interact? They can interact as richly and variously as any two people meeting anywhere; you have multiplied the possibilities.

3. You can start with an extant group: a family, a town, an enclave of almost any kind, and introduce almost anything:

a. A crisis: Ma, the natives are growing restless, Louie has appendicitis, our racehorse is spavined, the dam is bust.

b. A new character: the enemy, the stud from out of town who dazzles and upsets the women, the visiting relative.

c. A catalyst which changes existing relationships: coming of age of one of the characters, the introduction or removal of love; the introduction of something as sophisticated and elusive as a change of mood or as primitive and immediate as rage.

4. You can begin with characters in confrontation:

a. The love scene.

b. The parting.

c. The recognition scene.

d. The confrontation of the liar with truth or the truthful person with lies.

Each of these situations presupposes living characters, lines moving up to and away from the confrontation, some kind of resolution. I suspect there are as many possibilities as there are people and writers to write about them. The operative questions are: What has brought these people to this moment? What is going to happen now? What difference is it going to make?

It is also possible to depart from setting, the place and its effect on the people who are in it:

1. This place and how it defeats everybody who comes to it — e.g., the mental institution, the forest, the city, the haunted *house*, for heaven's sake, the hospital, anyplace . . .

2. This place and how it has defeated everybody who comes here except for X, who overcame it in these ways and for this reason.

3. This place and how it alters everybody who comes here: the couple who thought they loved each other, the cocksure kid who thought he knew everything, the confirmed failure who thought he was at the end of his life. The implication is that anybody introduced into this specific setting is going to come out with his opinion of himself reversed by what he encounters here.

4. This place and what happens to its people when they are forced to leave: the patient leaving the hospital, shaky and frightened; the country boy torn away from his beloved small town; the crew released from the confines of their ship or the prisoner from prison. The possibilities are endless.

It is also possible to work from institutions: church, state, schools, family, right on down to the Tuesday Afternoon Hydrangea Club.

1. The person who rebels against the institution.

2. The person who serves the institution and is well- or ill-treated as a result. This one can be a success story or a confrontation story, or even a story of pursuit and flight.

3. The person who brings change to the institution: the would-be president; the threatening new member with bizarre ideas; the one who sets the members to fighting among themselves; the one who has the others vying for his favors, which opens up possibilities for deceit and betrayal, of member and member, of members and new member, or members and new member and leader.

It is also possible to begin with ideas — not a Big Idea, but an idea as a point of departure:

What if a child is trapped overnight in a country fairground?

What if a spinster librarian falls in love with a teenaged boy?

What if a woman wakes up in the night to find her baby missing?

Such questions are perfectly respectable starting points, and having posed them you will find yourself faced with the same number and kind of decisions.

Maybe your story is going to grow out of a specific flash of vision, a captive moment: in interviews, Faulkner claimed more than once that he wrote *The Sound and the Fury* out of his vision of Caddy and her muddy drawers. If your story grows out of such a moment, or a mood or a vagrant flash of discovery, you can flesh it out by thinking backward: What has brought this person to this moment? What is going to happen now? What difference is it going to make?

There are hundreds of other possible points of departure, thousands of possibilities glittering in that alluvial sludge, waiting to be picked up and examined. Look at:

The mood a specific song evokes.

Any one of your dreams.

Remembered conversations, or overheard ones.

The thousands of snapshots memory makes.

The evocative qualities of certain small objects.

Shapes in landscapes.
People in landscapes.

Any one of these can be like the last step a diver takes before the plunge.

But whether you spin off from one of these ideas or begin to develop a story of your own, you'll want to know that something is really *happening*.

With this in mind, ask yourself at the outset, and again as you introduce every new character or a new turn in the story:

1. Who are these characters and what do they want?
2. What's at stake here?
3. What is the source of tension?

Like your characters, you need to care, and care passionately, about the answers, because you and your characters have to care enough about what's going on to draw in complete strangers — the unknown readers you want to interest in your story. They have to care enough to begin reading, and keep on reading until they've finished your story.

The stories which develop from your starting point can unfurl like ribbon or stretch wide and then tighten like nooses or describe an arc and go up to a high point and then quickly go down; they can spiral like a Slinky or gurgle into a vortex like the water down a bathtub drain, but they have one specific common characteristic: they developed naturally out of a chosen set of premises and they all have movement; they themselves move and they move the reader. A good story picks you up at one point and delivers you somewhere, even when it turns back in on itself and delivers you — somewhat changed by the experience — back at the beginning.

It is possible to talk about stories in terms of movement; some people like to talk about conflict and resolution but I think rather that readers need the sense after it's over that they've been somewhere or that something has happened, and that you as writer will have, rather, a sense of a shutter flexing and snapping, a certain satisfaction at the inevitability and fitness of things. I can't tell you how to accomplish this; as reader you will know it only in a secondary way, and you will not learn by following a mimeographed sheet of instructions or following the directions found in any book, even if I or somebody else could think up some for you. You will learn by reading enormous quantities of stories and by writing and writing until you recognize and feel these things for yourself.

Even the few simple possibilities I have listed seem formulaic in retrospect, and I think that, trying to anatomize the possibilities, I have made them seem cheap, which only confirms my suspicion that *the best stories make themselves from the inside out,* that the process has to be one of discovery, and the less we talk about it the better.

You can try *anything*. If it doesn't work, you have to be willing to try something else. This is the nature of writing.

Now that I think about it, it's probably a good thing I never found the fabled list of the lucky seven. If I stumbled onto it now, on a riverbank or buried in a casket at the bottom of the garden, I would give it a long regretful look and close the lid on it.

I wanted it, I looked for it for years, and at the last minute I found it and discovered that it wasn't what I wanted after all.

6

OUTLINE

nce you have a point of departure for your story, what comes next? Some writers are able to sit down and outline everything that is going to happen from the first scene to the last, with all the major events listed and everything else spelled out under neat headings and subheadings accompanied by notes on everything that is going to happen right down to the last line. They are able to say ahead of time what they are going to do and then sit down and do it by the numbers, one, two, three.

Others of us simply plunge in. For some of this second group the work will present itself as completely realized and well ordered as if there had been an outline. For the rest of us, writing fiction is like blundering in the dark; we work by trial and error, making choices and discoveries that create order. Only at the far end can we look back and tell you where we've been. We are a chauvinistic group, inclined to look with suspicion on writers with more orderly minds.

I used to believe that outlining could kill an idea deader than hitting it with a rubber mallet. After a season of working with student screenwriters, I have begun to think otherwise. Professional screenwriters begin with an outline—three or so pages that tell the whole story. The writer then proceeds to a fuller treatment, a scene-by-scene description of what is going to happen, when, where and how, describing the picture scene by scene down to the final frame. This treatment has to be complete and sound before the writer is ready to begin the screenplay.

This kind of outlining shortcuts a great many disasters. It forces the writer to think through the story in most respects before beginning to write it. He has to know who the characters are, the number and order of the scenes. Instead of problem-solving in process, as so many writers of fiction do, the screenwriter is forced to solve major narrative problems and make major narrative decisions ahead of time. Writing from an extended treatment, the writer has a detailed map of the territory before going into it.

Outlining may also narrow the possibilities for mystery, accidents and surprises, but it gives even as it takes away; it narrows the margin for error. If you are willing to fly blind you will indeed find a great many wonderful unforeseen things happening—but you also have to be prepared to throw away a great deal of what you write. There is a tradeoff involved, and there are writers on either side of the debate ready to fight to the death defending their own methods.

With that said, even those of us who court the mystery can see the advantages of the outline. Whether you prefer to outline and then write your story or apply outline to a story for diagnostic purposes, it provides you as writer with a crash course in completing your thinking.

1. It's cheaper to make a mistake in a one-page outline or a six-item list of mistakes than to spend hours, days, weeks on a story that won't work no matter what you do to it. If you begin listing the events in a story over and over and keep coming up short when you reach the crucial point, *with no idea what's going to fill the gap*, then it may be wiser to put your outline aside until it matures than to get stuck in the middle of a story with no resolution implied and none in sight.

2. Outline is a simple way to try out ideas, and to order and reorder the major events in a story or novel until your list seems *right*. Then you're ready to proceed because it's likely you have them in the right order.

3. If you have a story that isn't working you can use the outline for diagnostic purposes. You can:

a. Make a list of the events. Are they in the right order? Is there anything missing? Anything you can take off the list (remove from your story) to make the work more effective?

b. List the characters according to what each *wants*. Is this clear? How have you demonstrated this?

c. Try to identify the source of tension. Have you made it clear enough? If not, can you add an event or make an extant scene more dramatic to demonstrate this?

4. Outline is a clear aid to organization. Ordering and reordering your events, you'll develop a sense of what seems right for this particular story.

5. Even in mid-story you can sometimes use the outline to try out ideas as to What Comes Next. Number the events so far, One, Two, Three and if it's Four that has you baffled, try as many different entries under Four as you need to make your narrative decision. I'll show you how this works below.

Organizing and reorganizing, you can work with scissors and paste or a three-ring notebook with pages that can be reshuffled if you work by hand or by typewriter, or by shuffling files if you have a computer. Writers who have access to computers have tremendous mobility, and I can report from working with students that people who compose by computer are much more flexible about revision because they aren't facing the painful business of preparing a new typescript every time they make changes. It's possible to organize and reorganize lists and outlines and order and re-order scenes without the physical effort involved in producing a fresh copy from the ground up. I can suggest that you who work by hand or compose on the typewriter will profit by duplicating at a copy center so you can begin to edit and reorganize by cutting and pasting instead of having to recopy the whole thing. The added mobility is guaranteed to make you more flexible about rewriting, and when the time finally comes to retype or copy over your revision, it won't be nearly as painful.

Whether you proceed from an outline or write first and outline later, you need to think of the outline as one of the tools of the trade. It's there, it's cheap, it's available to everybody. Sooner or later, it's going to come in handy.

If you find your work profits from the preliminary outline, by all means begin there. You may still find that your story changes under your hands even as you write it. The important thing to remember is that the outline is not carved in stone. If accidents happen, be prepared to adapt to them. If a character arrives at a scene programmed to burst into tears and instead socks another character, or your story takes any other unexpected turn, you'll need to rethink your outline *from that point on* so that the story resolves itself in the light of this new development.

If you think you are an outliner, you may be able to use some suggestions.

1. If you can say in a sentence what your story is about, do it.
2. List your characters.
3. List the major scenes. Who is present? What happens?
4. Write down any other details you are sure of: time scheme, setting, anything else you know about the story.
5. Decide where you as narrator are going to stand. I treat this in detail in the next chapter.

Having done these things, you have made a number of major narrative decisions. Now you are ready to make an outline.

This could, I think, be short and simple: a one-page description or a diagrammatic numbering of scenes or sequences from beginning to end, or it could be a more elaborate numbering of scenes with full notes about what happens in each part of your story. If in the process of describing your first scene to yourself you find that you have begun writing your story, I'd suggest that it might be time to quit outlining and start writing.

At any level, from notes on the back of an envelope to a detailed treatment, outlining is, I think, the process of *discovering what you already know*. More than once I've run across a page of notes I didn't remember making — a single sheet of paper that I reread with surprise. Looking at it, I could see that this page of notes I had scratched out and put away and forgotten years before looked like an X-ray of one of my recent novels.

How did I know these things about the novel before I wrote it?

If I knew these things ahead of time, why was writing the novel so hard for me?

For me, at least, this has to do with process. I seem to need to proceed as if I don't know anything. In fact I don't really, or I don't know it all until after the book is written. Writing, I have to make all the same false starts and discoveries with every new work in order to get where I am going. If I were to outline in any kind of detailed way I would have to make all these mistakes and discoveries anyway. Outlining on a recent project, I wrote a dandy outline and then put it away and went ahead as if the outline did not exist. I seemed to need the surprises.

You may believe you are the same kind of writer. Even if you are, I have advice for you.

1. Take notes whenever they occur to you. Write them down on whatever comes handy and put them away. If you finish the piece you are writing without reference to them, go back and read them over before you call the story finished. Chances are what you have scribbled will appear in the story in some form. Sometimes the notes will show you the missing link in an exchange between characters, or give back a line of dialog better than the one that appears in the story.

2. If you are blundering around in a story, or have finished an early draft that doesn't work for one reason or another, stop and make a list of the scenes in your story — one or two words only — and number them. Let's say your list reads like this:

a. The meeting
b. The love scene
c. The fight
d. The parting
e. The betrayal

If the story isn't working, then you need to re-order the elements. Having reduced the elements in your story to this rudimentary level, you try moving them around. Maybe it goes:

a. The meeting
b. The love scene
c. The betrayal
d. The fight
e. The parting

Or maybe this seems better to you:

a. The meeting
b. The love scene
c. The fight
d. The betrayal
e. The parting

Or you decide to do away with (a), the meeting, altogether and merge the fight and betrayal or the fight and the parting. Standing off from your story after the fact, you are able to reduce it in this way because *the elements already exist*. List making helps you look at them more or less abstractly, in such a way that you are able to tell more easily whether events are occurring in the right order and, incidentally, how much of what you have is necessary to the story.

I am not suggesting that your story must contain any finite or specific number of elements or scenes. The temptation for many beginning writers is to assume that there are such formulae, or diagrams, or easy steps. This is not the case. It is, however, possible to break down a story you have written *after you have written it* and examine it carefully. It is also possible to make lists while in process: what you think is going to happen next, and in what order. What you need to remember is that lists change, even as outlines change, as you write, and that although outlining may give you an increased sense of control, no amount of list making or outline writing can replace the actual writing.

Questions About Outline

Planning a story, remember that an outline is a process available to help you complete your thinking. Then ask yourself:

1. Is this the kind of story that I can learn about through outline or am I going to have to start writing and ask these questions later?
2. Can I proceed from an outline and still stay flexible, or should I just keep notes on separate sheets of paper and be ready to shuffle the notes?
3. Do I need to outline to decide:
   a. the number and kinds of characters?
   b. The number and kinds of events?
   c. What comes first? That is, the order of events?
4. Can I use an outline to help me decide what to put in and what to leave out?
5. Can I use an outline to help me narrow narrative options once I come to a major turning point?
6. Can I use an outline to help me order and re-order events once my story is complete?

7

Point of View:
Playing by the Rules

*P*erhaps the single most important decision a writer makes at the beginning of a story is who the narrator is and where to stand. This decision casts itself in the first sentence and is more complex than it seems on first sight. In making it, the writer answers a surprising number of questions, and these answers lay down the ground rules for the story, beginning with the writer's own relationship to the characters and events. They will forecast the shape a story is going to take, and they will inform the style.

I don't think a writer beginning a story addresses these questions individually or sequentially. Each decision, beginning with whether to write in the first person or the third, precludes a number of others. The answers to all the questions present themselves in process, usually in less time than it will take me to separate and list them here. I believe these decisions are interwoven and more or less simultaneous, that a critical reader may need to separate them after the fact, but that a writer engaged in process does not.

At the same time, a beginning writer needs to be aware of the possibilities, simply because a writer must honor the specific set of decisions made for each story.

I have tried to sort out some of the questions:

1. Are you going to tell your story in the first person, the second (a rare and questionable bird which presupposes character for the reader), or the third?

2. If you are writing in the third person, how are you going to proceed?

a. Through a point-of-view character, or a set of point-of-view characters, seeing everything through their eyes?

b. As a detached observer—the fly on the wall or the microphone in the room, which observes and records but does not comment?

c. 'As an omniscient narrator, looking into the inner workings of the characters all at once, making judgments and explaining or interpreting for the reader?

In making this initial decision, you have already begun to cast the style. A story told by a first-person narrator assumes the diction of the speaker. You'll hear that person talking and you'll *know*.

I think a third-person scene viewed through a single character assumes certain rhythms according to the nature of the character and his moods. There is something simple, clear and detached about fly-on-the-wall third person, and, I think, something lordly about an omniscient narrator, something that lends a certain stateliness to the prose.

You've also answered in part questions as to how much your narrator knows. If you're working through a first-person narrator or a point-of-view character, the narrative is limited to what the character sees or finds out, or already knows. The fly on the wall knows what's going on within a given scene but can't move out of chosen scenes while they are going on or buzz away to see what's happening elsewhere or insinuate itself inside people's heads. The omniscient narrator can know it all.

3. To what degree is your first-person narrator or point-of-view character involved in what is going on?

a. If you are writing in the first person, is the narrator a participant or an observer? Is he talking about us, to whom this all happened, or them, to whom it happened as he watched, or did he hear about it all second hand piecing together the events to bring them to us?

b. If you are working through point-of-view characters, are they watching or taking part?

4. Where are you as writer standing in time?

a. Are all the events known as the story begins, so that you are telling it with hindsight ("If I had known then what I know now," or: "He could not know that within five years his fortune would be in ruins and Sarah dead of cancer")?

b. Or will the events discover themselves as you go along?

c. Does the story begin at the beginning or in the middle or even at the end, so that you are working backward to re-create events leading up to this high point?

d. If you begin at some high point, how will you handle information about what brought the characters to this moment? Flashbacks? Time shifts? Monologs? Exposition through dialog?

5. How does the first-person narrator or the point-of-view character know what he knows? How much does he know? If a first-person narrator, why and how is he telling us all this?

6. What about the tone, or manner? Is it comic or tragic or elegiac or matter-of-fact or what? This is going to reflect on the style, which will make itself felt in tone and manner, and all of this is controlled in part by all those other decisions.

This all sounds enormously complex and daunting to somebody sitting down to write a simple little story about people. The wonderful thing about it is that as you cast your first sentences, most of these questions automatically answer themselves, and once they are answered that multitude of options you faced before you began to write will narrow to a manageable range.

I was getting along fine with Mama, Papa-Daddy and Uncle Rondo until my sister Stella-Rondo just separated from her husband and came back home again. Mr. Whitaker! Of course I went with Mr. Whitaker first, when he first appeared here in China Grove, taking "Pose Yourself" photos, and Stella-Rondo broke us up. Told him I was one-sided. Bigger on one side than the other, which is a deliberate, calculated falsehood: I'm the same. Stella-Rondo is exactly twelve months to the day younger than I am and for that reason she's spoiled.

The story is Eudora Welty's "Why I Live at the P.O." and we know from the first sentence what the narrator is like because we hear the sound of her voice. We know this is her story, told firsthand from a certain vantage point; she is looking back on the events. She is directly involved in what went on and we can tell from her tone (which is comic and self-mocking but indignant) that she is a little bitter about it. All those questions were answered neatly and simply and it is unlikely that the author ever needed to confront them directly. She simply heard the narrator's voice, and let her talk.

George Garrett's story, "King of the Mountain," begins:

The time is the heart of the Depression and the place is Florida. Not the one you know about with white beaches and palm trees, orange-juice stands and motels, shuffleboards and striptease, amateur and professional, for young and old, all the neon glare and gilt of a carnival. This is at the center of the state where you might as well be a thousand miles from the unlikely ocean in long hot summer days, where in those days truck farmers and small-time ranchers grubbed for a living from the sandy earth or maybe planted and tended orange trees and hoped and sweated through the year for enough rain and, especially in winter, for warm weather, no frost.

Ask me why I pick that time and I'll tell you. There's a whole generation of us now, conceived in that anxious time, and if we're fat now, flash wide advertisement grins at the cockeyed careless world, we know still, deeply as you know the struggles of blood on the long pilgrimage of flesh, the old feel and smell of fear, the gray dimensions of despair, and, too, some of us, the memory of the tug and gnaw of being hungry.

The narrator is speaking with some regret from a time after the events are accomplished. His tone is elegiac and he has already let us know that this trip to the country was at least in part a trip into the past, and that it will probably end badly. We have a certain sense of him as educated, perceptive, thoughtful; we have begun to know him.

In "Barn Burning," Faulkner uses third person, working so tightly from within his point-of-view character that he is able to give us everything the boy thinks as well as everything he observes and takes part in. The rhythms are the rhythms of the character. For the moment we are in the present.

The store in which the Justice of the Peace's court was sitting smelled of cheese. The boy, crouched on his nail keg at the back of the crowded room, knew he smelled cheese, and more: from where he sat he could see the ranked shelves close-packed with the solid, squat, dynamic shapes of tin cans whose labels his stomach read, not from the lettering which meant nothing to his mind but from the scarlet devils and the silver curve of fish — this, the cheese which he knew he smelled and the hermetic meat which his intestines believed he smelled coming in intermittent gusts momentary and brief between the other constant one, the smell and sense just a little of fear because mostly of despair and grief, the old fierce pull of blood. He could not see the table where the Justice sat and before which his father and his father's enemy (*our enemy* he thought in that despair; *ourn! mine and hisn both! He's my father!*) stood, but he could hear them, the two of them that is, because his father had said no word yet:

"But what proof have you Mr. Harris?"

In "The Lottery," Shirley Jackson lets us as readers become the fly on the wall, observing without interpretation of characters' thoughts. We *see* rather than being told about their states of mind:

Mrs. Hutchinson craned her neck to see through the crowd and found her husband and children standing near the front. She tapped Mrs. Delacroix on the arm as a farewell and began to make her way through the crowd. The people separated good-humoredly to let her through; the two or three people said, in voices just loud enough to be heard across the crowd, "Here comes your Missus Hutchinson," and "Bill, she made it after all." Mrs. Hutchinson reached her husband, and Mr. Summers, who had been waiting, said cheerfully, "Thought we were going to have to get on without you, Tessie." Mrs. Hutchinson said, grinning, "Wouldn't have me leave m'dishes in the sink, now, would you, Joe?" and soft laughter ran through the crowd as the people stirred back into position after Mrs. Hutchinson's arrival.

"Well, now," Mr. Summers said soberly, "guess we better get started, get this over with, so's we can go back to work . . ."

Within the terms she has established, the author can tell us everything these people say and do while we are watching. She indicates inner states through external details, and limits herself *to this encounter as it takes place*.

It takes nerve to work this way because it is harder for the writer to focus, and to enlist reader sympathy. As readers and writers, we find it easy to take sides in a first- or third-person narrative in which we work through one character because we come to care about that character. The fly-on-the-wall technique gives evidence and leaves conclusions to the reader.

The omniscient narrator allows himself more latitude. Here is Joseph Conrad, in the opening of "An Outpost of Progress."

There were two white men in charge of the trading station. Kayerts, the chief, was short and fat; Carlier, the assistant, was tall, with a large head and a very broad trunk perched up on a long pair of thin legs. The third man on the staff was a Sierra Leone nigger, who maintained that his name was Henry Price. However, for some reason or other, the natives down the river had given him the name of Makola, and it stuck to him through all his wanderings about the country. He spoke English and French with a warbling accent, wrote a beautiful hand, understood bookkeeping, and cherished in his innermost heart the worship of evil spirits. . . . Makola, taciturn and impenetrable, despised the two white men . . . There was also another dwelling place some distance away from the buildings. In it, under a tall cross much out of the perpendicular, slept the man who had seen the beginning of all this; who had planned and had watched the construction of this outpost of progress. He had been, at home, an unsuccessful painter who, weary of pursuing fame on an empty stomach, had gone out there through high protections. He had been the first chief of that station. . . . Then, for a time, he dwelt alone with his family, his account books, and the Evil Spirit that rules the lands under the equator. He got on very well with his god. Perhaps he had propitiated him by a promise of more white men to play with, by and by. At any rate the director of the Great Trading Company, coming up in a steamer that resembled an enormous sardine box with a flat-roofed shed erected on it, found the station in good order, and Makola as usual quietly diligent. . . . The director was a man ruthless and efficient, who at times, but very imperceptibly, indulged in grim humor. He made a speech to Kayerts and Carlier, pointing out to them the promising aspect of their station. The nearest trading post was about three hundred miles away. It was an exceptional opportunity for them to distinguish themselves and to earn percentages on the trade. This appointment was a favor done to beginners. Kayerts was moved almost to tears by his director's kindness. . . . Kayerts had been in the Administration of the Telegraphs, and knew how to express himself correctly. Carlier, an ex-noncommissioned officer of cavalry in an army guaranteed from harm by several European powers, was much less impressed. If there were commissions to get, so much the better; and, trailing a sulky glance over the river, the forests, the impenetrable bush that seemed to cut off the station from the rest of the world, he muttered between his teeth, "We shall see, very soon."

Conrad has taken the whole canvas. He wants to be able to tell us everything about everybody: who they are, what happened to them before they came here, what they are thinking now. Later in the story he takes an even stronger hand, author speaking more or less directly to reader, telling us how to interpret the events:

Progress was calling to Kayerts from the river. Progress and civilization and all the virtues. Society was calling to its accomplished child to come, to be taken care of, to be instructed, to be judged, to be condemned; it called him to return to that rubbish heap from which he had wandered away, so that justice could be done.

In each case, the reader as outsider can see the answers to a number of major questions in the opening lines. My guess is that the writer as insider discovered even more answers, which unfold as the story goes along. Within the first few lines the rules for each story established themselves in such a way that the author knew what belonged and what didn't, what the rhythms and sequence would be, how the story would unfold.

First Person

Perhaps the most direct way to discover rules for a given story is to write in the first person. The gifts and limitations are apparent from the first line.

When I write in first person I will hear the voice first. Listening I know the character, male or female, what's the matter with him (let's say this one is male), what he *wants*.

The use of first person offers you as writer an opportunity for intimacy and full knowledge of character because you will become that character the minute he opens his mouth. It is an excellent device for beginning writers learning character, learning *anything*. You will know at once who the character is, how he is going to express himself, how he knows what he knows and how much he knows because, for the purposes of the story, you are that person. You will know what's the matter with him, what he wants.

Once you make that choice the rules simplify. The control is the speaker. His tone of voice sets the tone of the story. His diction and his observation and understanding of what is happening to him and the other characters will shape the story. You will know only what he already knows or will find out in the course of the story, and even then readers will hear only what he chooses to tell them, so that in part this choice solves the problem of what to put in and what to leave out. He will put the final gloss on what has happened in the story, and he always has the last word. The limitations are built in as surely as the advantages, but there is also a gift of certainty and safety.

Working from within a first-person narrator, you will know what he thinks, but you won't be able to go into the minds of the people he meets or hears about. He can surmise but he can never be sure. You can go where he goes, *but nowhere else.* You can see what he sees, *but no more.* You can learn what he learns, from experience or through hearsay or by reading documents left by others, *but nothing else.* Scenes are limited to the ones he plays firsthand, or remembers or imagines or hears about. You as writer are confined to the vision and opinions of this particular character, and depending on who he is and how skillful you are, you will find it like trying to move around in an Iron Maiden or you will wear him like a second skin, living your story firsthand.

Even knowing what you do when you become that person telling his story, you will need to discover more. Because real fiction brings its own set of convictions and can't be tampered with in this way, I'll ring the changes on a simple example *constructed for this purpose.*

First, where is this person standing? Does he know past, present and future before he begins to talk, and how much is he going to tell the reader? The simplest decision is to assume for the purposes of the story that he knows only what is going on while it's going on, and to tell the story from the beginning:

> I walked into Greeble's Dry Goods Store to discover everybody in the place staring at me. There was a lean, ugly-looking guy backed into the racks of women's housedresses and he was holding a rifle. It was pointed at me.

Narrator knows what is happening because it is happening to him. He may tell it with a certain amount of humor but there is an urgency because that really is a gun and it really is pointed at him. The remaining major decision can be made at the end of the story: if it's about the narrator and the bandit with the rifle, whom he vanquishes, we can end with the defeat of the bandit or we can take a jump in time and end years later, with the narrator telling the whole thing from the front porch of a rest home, or we can end with the simple sentence "Then he raised the gun and pulled the trigger," implying that our hero got his, which raises the question: Where is he telling us all this *from?* This will not be hard to decide from the vantage point of the end of the story in which everything has happened chronologically and the rest is already known.

Another possibility would be to assume a relevant past and tell the story in the linear present:

> I walked into Greeble's Dry Goods Store to discover everybody in the place staring at me. Greeble didn't want to tell me what was going on but

I leaned on him a little and he let me know that Lafe Jackson was out of prison and he was looking for me. He seemed to think it served me right for turning Lafe in after the robbery.

All the groundwork is laid for a tense story about pursuit and flight without further reference to the past, unless the narrator wants to brood about it or Lafe wants to bellyache about it when he captures our hero.

On the other hand, the narrator may want to use the knowledge of past, present and future all at once, telling his story in that maddening way many real-life storytellers use, dropping hints along the way, circling the material and going off on tangents, saving the punchline (which may even be something that happened before the story began) for the end, when listeners (in this case, readers) are rocking faster and faster because the suspense is unbearable. This method can be used to evocative and elegiac effect, impressing readers with the mystery and complexity of life, or it can be used in more homely ways, to build suspense and at the same time create impatience in the reader who is depending on this narrator who knows the answers but is determined to tell it *his* way, with gestures, instead of coming right to the point.

By the time I reached Greeble's that day I knew Lafe Jackson was looking for me, Lafe whom I had wrestled in the swamp the night they took him away, and whom I would wrestle again before the day was out. How could any of us know then what the terrible consequences would be for Lafe, for Rosalind, for me?

The narrator is hinting at a complete body of knowledge from the past, along with what is happening at the time the story opens, and he is also letting you know from the beginning that he knows exactly how the story will end. From that base he can move into past scenes between him and Lafe, him and Rosalind, hint at something between Lafe and Rosalind (what he thinks happened) and he can use all those people in the present at the same time, intercutting scenes with glimpses or intimations of the future, in which the passions and complications of the past and the pain of the present are altered, slightly, by what is to come. The possibilities are almost endless, they will make a richer story, but the dangers are greater; the whole thing can go out of control in a matter of seconds.

Perhaps the tightest control comes in a story told by the narrator as it unfolds. He doesn't know what is going to happen and can only tell it in stages:

I am in my room now, I just came from Greeble's, Lafe Jackson lunged at me from out of nowhere, Lafe, that I thought was dead. He would have killed me but Greeble was there, he threw himself between us and bought me a little time, but in case he gets me next time, I want to leave some kind of record.

Unless the writer assumes an omnipresent listener, the premise is that the narrator is keeping a diary or telling his story to a tape recorder. The function of the device is to tell a story in which the narrator is in suspense even as the reader is. The approach gives a certain spontaneity and velocity to the story, but the limitations are clear. The narrator has no foreknowledge and so the shape his story takes will be controlled by events; he is limited in time, place and action, as the story stands or falls on his ability to stop the action long enough to gasp out the next stanza, and he has to be able to make those pauses so naturally that readers can't object.

At the same time you are making those choices about time, you as writer will decide where the narrator figures in the story; whether he is a central character, a functioning peripheral character or only a member of the chorus. In the examples above, the narrator is a central character.

In the following, he is not:

When I went to Greeble's that day I had no way of knowing that Lafe Jackson was on the loose, or that he was looking for Randolph, although I should have guessed it, or what the two of them would do because of Rosalind. We all knew there was bad blood between them, but none of us knew how bad.

This is a narrator at a comfortable distance, snugly set in the community and observing the action. In this example, he is only an observer, and incidentally, he knows it all before he begins to tell us.

Perhaps your narrator is a secondary character, who was there, but in a peripheral way. He could function in some of the same ways in which Nick Carraway figures in *The Great Gatsby*, the observer who is engaged with the central figures, in love with the girl but doomed not to loom very large in any of their lives:

I was there in Greeble's when Lafe Jackson first took out after Randolph, I wanted to jump in and stop Lafe but there were arms and legs and blood flying and no way to get at the tangle, so I went and stood with Rosalind and tried to shield her, it was the only time I ever touched her. She was crying and didn't even notice but I will never forget that day.

This is a narrator who is emotionally involved but secondary to the action, watching from behind the counter or hiding behind a display of number ten orange juice cans.

No matter where your first-person narrator stands, you will have to know how he gets his information. He can know because it all happens or is happening to him, or he can know because he sees it happening to somebody else. In either case, he will be present for all the scenes. He can know what happens when he isn't there because people have told him about it, or because he has gone around after the fact, ferreting out details, or because he has read about it, or through a combination of any or all of the above. He can even tell you what he *thinks* happened.

Other characters can come in and tell him about it: "Lafe is at the station now, Ralph says he's killed Sim Watkins and a couple of others and now he's looking for you." He may read anything he can get his hands on: " 'I hate that snivelling bastard,' it said, right there in Lafe's own hand. 'He lied about me doing the murder because he wanted to get his hands on Rosalind.' Naturally I decided to burn the note."

He can listen to the radio or pick up the papers:

KILLER VOWS DEATH
TO STATE WITNESS

or he can read trial transcripts. Or he can observe the action from a safe distance, crouched behind the counter or watching from across the street as the fight rolls out onto the sidewalk. Hiding in the bushes, he can watch Lafe with the girl, overhearing a little, assuming what is going through their minds. Hearing that they have met, he can even speculate on what must have taken place between them.

In the old days, writers working in the first person found it necessary to use framing devices: the discovery of a document, a conversation between travelers leading to one traveler's story, or a character's decision to keep a journal or make a written account of some extraordinary things that just took place. These possibilities are still legitimate, but we grew up with instant images and disembodied voices and we are ready to accept stories which simply begin. As writers, we are willing to assume that the narrator simply began to talk, or write, at the moment we began to write this story. If a particular story demands a device, we may use devices ranging from the tape recorder to the manuscript found in a bottle, or let our characters *remember*.

Third Person

Working in the third person through a point-of-view character offers some of the same kind of intimacy and control, but at the same time it gives the writer more flexibility.

You will need to know all the same things about your point-of-view character that you would about a first-person narrator: where he is standing in time; whether he is involved in what's going on, and if so, how deeply; how he knows what he knows. It would be a simple matter to take each one of those ways of writing a first-person story about Lafe and Rosalind and Randolph and render them in the third person. It would work because a point-of-view character functions in most of the same ways, and the limitations imposed in terms of time scheme, involvement and the ways this character knows things are similar.

At the same time:

1. The writer has the added ability *to see the character from the outside*: you can describe the character's looks and aspect as opposed to or indicative of inner states.

2. The writer can draw the scene before the character walks into it: what the place looks like, what the other people are doing, and can do so with greater art than a writer could in the character of a person telling a story. Although more limited than when using an omniscient narrator, the writer has mobility of vision.

3. The writer can pick up subtleties the character may not notice *at the time*: attitudes on the part of other characters, innuendo, speeches made when the point-of-view character isn't really listening.

4. There is a greater opportunity for flights of style. This is linked with mobility of vision, but there is another factor. Although the writer assumes a character's way of looking at things, *there's no limitation created by the character's diction or his vocabulary*.

When I work in the third person, I seem to need to work through a point-of-view character. Although the story told in the third person may not have the rush and immediacy of an outcry or a threnody or an aria by a first-person narrator, the advantages are enormous. I know at once who I am for the purposes of the story. I can engage the reader with my central character because I am engaged with her. Once I know her, I have discovered a major factor in the inner logic of the particular story. The problem of focus is solved at the same time as the problem of what to put in and what to leave out. As writer, I can give more about what is going on than my central character can take in; because I am the narrator and she is not, I can tell more about a scene than she might want to tell if she were telling the story herself. Because I am working from within her, I am not tempted to wander into other characters' minds while I tell her story. The obvious limitation is that I can't tell the reader what other characters are thinking and I can't give scenes where this character is not present.

Here is an example from a long work which follows a single character. In this scene Willard Michaels has made up his mind to leave a place where he has been miserable. The women are his landlady and the mother of one of his students. Weidemeyer is the principal of the high school where he has been teaching. The novel is *Captain Grownup*.

As he packed, Mrs. LaZar's decor seemed to be pursuing him, with crocheted doilies leaping for his sleeves and the gray-pink shag rug pulling at his feet like quicksand, miring him in this small town. He had to act fast and so he took down the full color reproduction of Van Gogh's *Starry Night*, striking a blow for freedom with Magic Marker in two colors on the dingy wall. He was pleased with the results: a combination of the Martyrdom of St. Sebastian, the Primavera and the Battle of the Bulge, and he wrote, at the bottom: The Good Taste Vigilantes *Strike*, and then, a lifelong victim of insuperable politeness, stopped to write the good lady a check.

"Michaels, there you are."

"There he is, the bastard. What have you done with my daughter?"

"What have you done to my wall?"

Pushing the women aside, Hal Weidemeyer stepped forward to confront him, righteous brown nose in brown suit. "What do you have to say for yourself?"

Michaels set his suitcase down on Weidemeyer's foot. "Would you believe goodbye?"

So long as Michaels is in the scene I am free to give you all the lines and directions for all the characters. I can tell you everything Michaels is thinking and what I know about him because I am with him and I can give you a pretty good idea what the others are thinking by assigning them stage directions. Weidemeyer is acting righteous and Michaels thinks he is a brown nose, so I can tell you those things without ever jumping into Weidemeyer's mind. I can't tell you what all those people are going to do after Michaels drives out of sight, although I can tell you what they are doing as he bolts down the steps and away from them, even though he isn't watching. I can't tell you what these people were doing before they landed in his apartment, either, although I know. What I can do is make it apparent that the mother is furious because her daughter is missing and the landlady is upset about her damaged wall. I am much freer than I would be if I let Michaels tell the story, because he would be too agitated to notice everything I notice, and too embarrassed to report most of it. I can use more complicated language than he would use if he were to report to you firsthand, and I'm much more accurate than he would be at reporting dialog. At the same time, I have access to his thoughts alone, and I can go where he goes and nowhere else. In this particular piece of work I used letters to and from Michaels and a couple of flashbacks involving Michaels to broaden scope. Showing him in scenes with other characters, both old friends and new acquaintances, I could give the reader some idea what other characters thought of him.

The other possibility for me, working in the third person through a point-of-view character, is to shift from character to character according to the scene. In an early novel, I am with the girl Willie in all the scenes where she is present, with her grandmother when she is not present, with an aging lecher called Davenport Carlyle in scenes which don't involve the others, and with his sadist nephew Emil only in scenes where Emil is alone. Emil is a repulsive character and better seen through and by others, in terms of their responses to him. When I am alone with him I will deal with him through external actions because I don't want reader sympathy for him. Because I am following given characters, I have the mobility necessary to tell the reader everything I want, and I can have things going on behind people's backs. I can give scenes in which everybody is present and to the reader they may appear more or less panoramic, but I am with Willie.

In this scene we are in a Florida hotel, where Anna Snigg has brought Willie, her fifteen-year-old granddaughter. Except for Willie and Emil, everybody is old. The novel is *Mother Isn't Dead She's Only Sleeping*.

Willie dreaded the dining room. She scrubbed off her lipstick and pulled her hair back in a knot, but she knew before she started across the room to the table that she couldn't foil the old men. Their eyes were on her the minute she appeared in the stucco arch. She faltered a minute, but before she could duck behind a pillar and escape, her grandmother saw her and nodded imperiously from the table, and Willie held her breath and plunged into the room. . . . When she reached the table where her grandmother sat toying with a martini, Willie pulled out a chair and, in a movement that was half accidental, stepped hard on Davenport Carlyle.

"Well, *there* you are," he said, pretending not to wince. His ruddy face was ruddier than usual, with a flush that traveled through the roots of his thin, wavy white hair. After Willie was seated, he shook his injured leg surreptitiously. When Willie ducked under the table to retrieve her napkin she noted that there was a small fleck of blood growing larger on the shin of his white silk sock. She planted her elbows on the table and smiled.

"Well, here we are," said Anna Snigg with a little shiver.

"Yes," Carlyle said tiredly. "Here we are." And he turned his attention to the menu.

The headwaiter appeared, and Anna watched him apprehensively. Then Carlyle inclined his head ever so slightly and the small miracle of command was worked again. As the man stood, still bent in a bow, Carlyle bent his head over Anna's menu and helped her with the French.

Awed by the grace with which he approached his dinner, Anna ate as if she were following a demonstration, picking up each new piece of silver a split second after he did, using her napkin with the same flourish, finishing with the same delicate pat. . . .

Willie was too tired and too preoccupied to notice the silence at the table, or the way Carlyle's neck went in and out, or the way her grandmother kept plucking at her plum-colored bodice with an unsteady smile. She turned with relief to her own thoughts, speaking politely when she was spoken to, grateful that the old people's talk wasn't as obtrusive as usual and that they weren't calling on her much at all. A creepy feeling at the back of her neck pulled her to attention, and she saw Emil turn and sidle away from the dining-room door. Carlyle suddenly snapped forward in his seat and began pressing Anna Snigg with compliments, and Willie wondered at the change in the tempo and quality of the conversation, unaware of the expression Emil had worn just before she looked up and saw him, or the gesture he had made toward Davenport Carlyle.

This treatment is close to panoramic, but whether or not you noticed it, I was with Willie the whole time. The only mind I went into was hers, and everybody else's actions and moods were externally observed. I was able to show things going on in the room that Willie might not have noticed, and I had the range to show, firsthand, every thing except what the others were actually thinking. For me, working through Willie offered an opportunity to narrow the options for what I was going to put in and leave out, and to focus the story and the reader's attention on the heroine. Everything that is going on in the room is considered as it will affect her. When I cut to Davenport and Emil in another scene, the reader finds out, without Willie knowing, what plans they have for her.

It is possible, within the framework of this kind of third person, to give a considerable amount of what the central character is thinking. A made-up example would be:

Watching Elise, he remembered all the times they had been together, when she had responded to him and when she had not, and just exactly which chords she had struck in him when they were both young. Now they were both aging, and he had the idea that he was aging faster than she was. He had a sense of all their losses and their best time passing, and at this moment, when he wanted most to talk to her, she was busy packing her suitcase and wouldn't look at him.

Although I am writing in the third person, with the gift of detachment available if I want it, I can go as far into the leading character's thoughts as I want to without disturbing the reader's concentration. I could not then add, "Elise was thinking he looked particularly pouched and ugly this morning, and she wished he would leave," because I have decided to follow him throughout and jumping into Elise's mind would be breaking the rules. I would, however, feel perfectly comfortable adding, "He had no way of knowing that Elise was thinking he looked pouched and ugly this morning, and wished he would leave." It's sneaky but I would feel justified because I am still working within his frame of reference: what he knows and can't know. I would be more likely to get at what she thinks and feels through her actions and dialog.

Having had access to my character's thoughts, I would find it difficult to pull back to the position of that fly on the wall, but other writers do so to great effect.

In the opening of "Red Leaves," Faulkner watches and listens to two Indians:

The two Indians crossed the plantation toward the slave quarters. Neat with whitewash, of baked soft brick, the two rows of houses in which lived the slaves belonging to the clan, faced one another across the mild shade of the lane marked and scored with naked feet and with a few homemade toys mute in the dust. There was no sign of life.

"I know what we will find," the first Indian said.

"What we will not find," the second said. Although it was noon, the lane was vacant, the doors of the cabins empty and quiet; no cooking smoke rose from any of the chinked and plastered chimneys.

"Yes. It happened like this when the father of him who is now the Man, died."

"You mean, of him who was the Man."

"Yao."

The first Indian's name was Three Basket. He was perhaps sixty. . . . Clamped through one ear Three Basket wore an enameled snuff-box.

The author follows his characters through this scene as impersonally as a fly traveling with them, and he records dialog as if he had a microphone concealed inside that snuffbox. In the next scene he will pull back to a position of omniscience but for the time being the approach is external and we are allowed to see and hear without being told what to think.

The effect is cinematic, realistic. The prose will be crisp and direct and scenes rendered this way are always swift. The limitations are built in. The fly on the wall cannot know what has gone before unless the characters tell him, nor can he know what people are thinking, what is happening elsewhere, what is going to happen.

Before his death John O'Hara was one of the nation's leading practitioners of this technique. His dialog passages present themselves on the page like no one else's, and an extraordinary detachment marks all his work. Even when he purports to follow a central character, his dialog scenes unfold as if for a hidden microphone. From *The Lockwood Concern*:

". . . Did Grossvater give me the pony?" George asked his mother.

"You might say he did."

"But did he?"

"You might say so. Why do you care, as long as you got it?"

"Because I want to tell Davey."

"Well—no. Poppa and I gave you the pony, but Grossvater gave me the money for my share, so you might say he gave you the pony too."

"But do I have to thank Grossvater too?"

"No, you don't have to thank him."

"Then he didn't give it to me, or you'd make me thank him."

"You're like your Poppa. You can twist around with your questions. Just don't say any more about it."

Davey Stokes, when he got his pony, told George that their Grossvater had not bought it, that it had been bought by his parents, and that Leroy Hoffner was getting one from *his* parents. "Grossvater is a big liar," said Davey Stokes.

"He's a dumb-Dutch big liar, that's what my father says. My father says all the Dutch are stingy."

"Your mother's Dutch."

"Not any more."

"She talks Dutch."

"She does not," said Davey Stokes. "My father won't let her. . . ."

The fly has buzzed out of one scene, between George and his mother, and right into another, between George and Davey. The cutting is so quick and skillful that the reader is moved from one place to another without questioning how he got there or what happened in between. O'Hara scenes, like certain Hemingway scenes, are so swift as to be almost abstract. At the same time, the reader is in sure hands, and what is presented is so economically done and apparently accurate that there is no time to raise questions.

The next remove is to omniscience. The writer will use everything the characters think, exercising optimum mobility to take the reader from character to character, taking the added liberties of interpretation and foreknowledge. Although this seems to me to be a cooler technique, it enables the writer to know everything and tell everything about a given story and the characters in it. In his novel *Slow Motion Riot*, Peter Blauner, a new novelist, pulls back to show us all the characters in a given scene:

"Why y'all beeping me when I'm talking to my probation officer?" Darryl King wanted to know.

"How do I know who you're talking to?" said his sister Joanna Coleman, looking up from the horoscope chart on her refrigerator. "All I know is that I got business to discuss with you right away."

She wore a gold cable as big as an arm around her throat. Two brown incense sticks burned on the kitchen table, wafting a sweet, overpowering odor through the room, and there was a "healing" crystal on top of the refrigerator. A pile of self-help and astrology books sat on the counter.

Joanna's two children, Howard, the six-year-old boy, and LaToya, the five-year-old girl, were running around the cramped apartment like wild Indians. The boy was like a little man. He walked around with a stern expression and his shoulders back, turning his body from side-to-side as if he was ready for a fight at any angle. The little girl followed him, with her pig-tails flapping. She threw her arms over her little brother's shoulders like she wanted him to give her a ride.

"LaToya, you mind your brother," her mother warned her. "Else he'll turn around and smack you one. . ."

Aaron Williams, the 14-year-old with the harelip, sat on the sofa, watching the Mets game on the television. Darryl's large friend Bobby "House" Kirk sat next to him and a catatonic-looking boy Darryl had never seen before sat on the floor staring at Bobby's size 16 sneakers.

"What's so important?" Darryl asked.

"Him," his sister Joanna said, pointing to the catatonic boy. She said his name was Eddie Johnson and he was sixteen years old. Darryl King glanced over at him. The boy had hair that stood straight up and no physical energy. He was like a piece of furniture. Joanna explained that Eddie Johnson usually woke up at noon every day and sat up in bed about two hours later. By early evening, he'd come as far as the front room where he watched until it was time to go to sleep again.

"They think he's depressed," said Joanna.

"So what?" Darryl said.

"But he listens good," his sister told him. "That's the thing. You say something he hears it. He never forgets it. He notice everything . . . Even though he's a Scorpio . . ."

Darryl glared at the blank-faced boy on the sofa. Then he clapped his hands in disgust and pivoted away from all of them. "Joanna, I don't believe you called my beeper for this . . ."

Working at a long enough distance to allow him to deal with what's going on with everybody in the apartment more or less all at once, Blauner has left himself the freedom to go in and out of Darryl's mind at will, and in other parts of the novel, deals with any number of other characters and what they're thinking.

Although most writers follow a single set of rules within the framework of a short story, they will work with a wider range of possibilities in a novel. If you sit down to examine the techniques employed in a novel written in the third person, you are likely to find that the author employs more than one of these modes. A novelist committed to one character may pull back to give group scenes and confrontations, becoming as detached and faithful as that fly on the wall. The faithful recorder may find it necessary to pull back to a position of omniscience because in certain scenes the reportorial technique is insufficient. The omniscient narrator may move in for fly-on-the-wall close-ups of certain scenes and at times may move into one character for several pages at a time, in effect giving the reader entire scenes through a single point-of-view character.

Some writers looking for the best of all possible worlds will employ a technique I call "mixed media." This happens more often in the novel than in the short story, but the technical boundaries of the short story are flexing and expanding even as I write, and accomplished writers as varied as Faulkner and Tillie Olsen have employed this particular technique. Mixed media intersperses third-person narrative with monologs by one or more characters. When a skillful writer does this, the possibilities increase geometrically. It is possible to give major characters monologs or threnodies, arias or laments which are interspersed with third-person narrative, or to intercut monologs by several different speakers, each with his distinctive tone of voice, or to give one character's first-person account of events and then set it against a cool account of what "really" happened, or to juggle and intercut past, present and future, using diaries and letters and passionate outcries and bits of memory — whatever seems right.

I should add that the more ambitious the technique, the broader the possibility of failure, but that's true of any great adventure. My best advice to any writer just beginning to work in the short story is to learn how to control a relatively straightforward first- or third-person narrative before launching into more complex, uncharted territory. The results are rich and complicated, and the limitation, if there is one, is in the area of focus — knowing the center of your story and making the reader know it. Technique will never give a center to a story which has no center, and you as beginning writer risk losing track of your story, what you're really trying to tell, and leaving your reader at sea without a compass or even a star to navigate by. It takes a skilled writer in full command of all talents to control a narrative once it's been opened out in this manner.

A writer just beginning to make fiction will discover within the first few lines of a story how quickly the rules make themselves. You may find it simplest to begin working in the first person, because first person supplies an immediate sense of character, of what does and does not belong in the story, and it solves problems of intimacy and focus. If you work in third person, through a point-of-view character, you will keep most of those advantages, adding mobility and flexibility. The third person fly-on-the-wall narration offers a different kind of mobility, but sacrifices a certain degree of intimacy, both with the characters and with the reader. The writer can detail everything about a certain group of characters within a given setting—everything, that is, except what they are thinking, how they really feel. The omniscient narrator sees all and tells all, but focus is more difficult to achieve, and as writer employing this technique you will not be as close to your characters or your readers as a writer working from within a single character because you haven't taken sides.

Deciding Where to Stand

If you have an idea for a story and want to get started but can't decide where to stand, ask yourself:

1. Do I hear anything? Complete sentences? If the answer is yes, then even without knowing it, you've fallen into the narrative manner *for this story* and are ready to begin. If not, ask yourself:

2. How can I best tell this story? If the answer doesn't immediately present itself, you may need to press yourself to a decision by asking:

3. Am I comfortable with first person? Can I fall into character and stay there for the duration of my story, and if I do, is this the best way for me to tell the story?

a. Who is this character and do I know what I as this character sound like?

b. Am I comfortable with this character's vocabulary and tone of voice?

c. Can I sustain it?

d. Are there things I want to tell that this character can't possibly know about?

e. Where is this character standing in time?

f. Am I as character telling the story as it unfolds, or recollecting in tranquillity?

g. Am I as narrator involved in the story or am I only an observer?

h. If I'm only an observer, do I deserve to be the narrator?

4. What about third person?

a. Who is my point-of-view character? Is there more than one? Which of my characters sets the narrative tone?

b. Do I want to use my point-of-view character as a pseudo-first person, working so tightly that the whole story is colored by this character's perception, or:

c. Do I want to let my character function as a camera, recording without judging?

d. Do I want to step back a little farther and move between several characters as an omniscient narrator?

Notice how the answers to these questions will shut out some narrative options for this particular story and open others to you. By the time you come up with the answers, you're well on your way into your story.

Even skimming the surface of this chapter, you can see the territory is rich and promising. When you decide, for the purposes of a given story, who you are and where you are going to stand, you will see the rules make themselves as if by magic. You have already narrowed the options to a manageable number. Once you begin to write you will understand firsthand how quickly the remaining questions answer themselves. Writing, you will *know*.

8

VOICES: WRITING DIALOG

"*I*f you don't keep still I'm going to smack you, Daddy's never going to let us in with you hollering like that, I didn't drive eight hundred miles to have Daddy lock us out. It's all your fault he left us anyway, now hush!"

You may not recognize her immediately, but I know her. She's thirtyish, skinny, overly made up and underbred. I think she and the boy are sitting in a Howard Johnson's outside a major city, with plastic plants waving in all the flower boxes and semis roaring by outside.

"Fat lot you know, now lay *off*."

He may be crying, but he's tough.

"Look what you did, you got ketchup on me. John Henry, *please* don't make me cry." She's not as tough as she seems.

"Madam, I wonder if you and your little boy would lower your voices. Please, you're disturbing the other customers. Madam, what are you doing to that child?"

This is the hostess. She is an older woman; a younger one might not even notice the scene and she would never intervene. She is, on the surface, gracious and genteel, but she is upset by the conflict; in trying to stop it, she has broken restaurant protocol. She has, furthermore, invaded the pair's privacy. The boy will tell her.

"Get away, lady, you leave my momma alone."

I hear a character coming even before I see him. The minute he opens his mouth I know him: what he looks like, the way he moves. The minute another person enters the scene and speaks I know who she is, what's the matter with both of them, what they *want*. In the hypothetical scene in the restaurant, I have already found out who the people are; I think I know what the boy did to drive the father away from home — I think he made a slip of the tongue that let Daddy know his wife was being unfaithful. Once I know what happened the day Daddy ran away, I will know him too, and so I can begin to predict his response to this pair when they finally catch up with him.

Another scene.

"My dear, you may think you know Stanley, but I might as well warn you now, his interest in you will never equal his interest in his work. If you want a full-time husband, I suggest you fish in other waters."

The speaker is in his late fifties, cultivated, probably an academic. I think he resents Stanley's interest in this young woman because Stanley has been spending too much time with her and not enough on his work. If his resentment stems from a deeper kind of jealousy, he does not even suspect it.

"I'll take Stanley any way I can get him. If I have to, I'll club him and drag him out of that library by his hair."

The young woman is blunt and forceful. She is not frightened of the older man nor is she impressed by his condescending air.

"I think you will find those tactics do more harm than good. Stanley has never cared much for brute force."

"I don't think you know what Stanley cares for. You never bothered to find out."

"If you take him off this project you'll have reason to regret it, my dear."

"Don't worry, John, I'll marry him and return him safe and sound the very next morning. He won't miss a day."

Even hypothetical scenes take life the minute the characters begin to speak. Dialog is the life of fiction, lighting character from within, bringing life and drama to scenes as they unfold, opening new doors.

Raw dialog comes as naturally as thought. Most writers hear voices all the time. Characters speak and they *become*.

This is only part of the process. The other is distillation. You will not make fiction with any skill until you are willing to engage in this other part of the process: controlling and refining those voices, distilling speech to make fiction.

A writer is never alone for long. The house may be empty but it is never really silent because every writer hears a distinctly personal collection of voices: remembered conversations, imagined dialogs and great undelivered speeches, disembodied fragments, catch phrases and memorable lines. There are always distant tunes sounding: rinky-tink melodies, fugues, arias, entire quintets waiting to be recorded. There is always at least one character rattling around at the fringes of the writer's consciousness, clamoring.

Listen and you can hear them: "Listen to *me*."

When you bring that person to the page you won't take down the speeches verbatim. Although you are all of your characters, there are already changes taking place. When this one speaks, the lines are going to sound like the character's, not yours.

For the writer, the distilling process begins in the subconscious; it must be completed in process, perhaps in a series of written drafts, before speech can become fiction.

All of us begin with those great undelivered speeches, the imagined dialogs between us and the tough kid or the unfair teacher or the beautiful person we want to know better. At the same time those of us who are writers are listening, recording, so that both sets of voices, imagined and remembered, settle down somewhere in that alluvial sludge, humming until we are ready to draw on them.

As a writer I am given to fits of insomnia, usually after evenings with new people or old friends who have said something new, or said something differently. This used to make me restless and fitful. I would wander around popping aspirin or animal crackers or breathing deeply at an open window or using one of the old routines: "Now the muscles in my big toe are relaxed, soon the muscles in the rest of the toes will relax, and then the feet, then the ankles, then the knees . . ." I was convinced wakefulness was an aberration; after all, everybody else in the house was asleep.

It took me some years to understand that aspirin and animal crackers were not the answer because I was suffering the effects of an occupational hazard. I was working.

I was playing my tapes. This might be a repulsive habit if I did it intentionally. It makes me seem calculating, unprincipled, stealing bits of people's speech without their knowing it. The simple truth is that I can't help it. With or without aspirin and animal crackers, I am going to be awake until the last interesting exchange or riveting recital or fight or moment of high comedy has replayed itself and the good bits have settled into that alluvial sludge. When it's over I can sleep — not before.

At the same time I want my friends and relations and those people at the disastrous dinner party to relax because none of what they said is going to emerge whole, and when it does emerge they aren't going to recognize it because whatever they said does not belong to them any more. It's mine. When it emerges from the mouth of that character who's battering at me and trying to make me listen, it will be at one more remove: it will be his.

Writing dialog is not simply a matter of collecting speeches and assigning them to characters, nor is it a matter of recording speech and transmitting it whole. Part of learning speech is listening; another part is forgetting what you've heard. I know a nice old lady who is keeping a notebook. She is doggedly writing down "all the crazy things you hear people say." When she finishes, she will have a lovely collection of funny things to read to her friends, but this is not fictional dialog, nor is she a writer.

Listening to all those voices, a writer remembers not actual speech but the *truth* of speech. Playing my tapes and grappling with insomnia, I know the time this takes is not the same as actual time elapsed. Instead, I'm re-hearing the best of the conversation; I've already begun to distill.

When a writer tells a story at a party, he has already carried the process another step. Telling you about the time he got stuck in the elevator with the Austrian lion-tamer, he will do the accent and pretend that he is giving you the exchange verbatim, but what he gives you is not precisely what he heard.

He has left out the boring parts, the ums and ahs, the asides about the weather and the number of times the lion-tamer asked whether he thought the elevator was really only stalled or whether there was a citywide power failure and they were going to be stuck there for days. Instead he'll give you the line about the power failure once and skip right to the good part: when the lion-tamer burst into tears and he, the writer, said bravely, "Do not worry, Adolpho, I will save you." Even in cocktail party conversation, he will distill.

A friend, a distinguished novelist, once dictated a novel to a stenographer. The work was mostly dialog, and in saying every line aloud, he wanted to get closer to the truth of everyday speech. He took all the parts, playing each scene naturally, as it unfolded. When he was finished and his stenographer handed him the transcription, he looked at it and tore it up. There was no art involved in this particular work and it had no life. He knew that to achieve not dialog but the *truth* of dialog, he would have to see the work on the page, to work as he always did. He couldn't just let it happen; he would have to choose, discard and shape.

This is because dialog is never everyday speech transmitted directly to the page. It is not even the best of the best, as the writer absorbs and remembers it. It is speech ordered and distilled, speech which moves in a straight line instead of circling and doubling back on itself as so much real conversation does. It is speech without all the uhs and ahs and digressions and repetitions people use when they meet and talk.

What's more, I'm convinced that those voices we hear, characters rattling around trying to make us listen, seldom deliver finished dialog.

Usually they say too much. I'll take another made-up example to give you the bare bones and an idea of what does and does not belong on the skeleton.

Pretend I've written a scene in which John tells Mary he is leaving her forever. I am likely to find that I've written three or four unnecessary exchanges leading up to the central action. In a first draft, I had to let them rattle on until I was sure what they were getting at and how they were going to arrive at the central moment of drama. In reworking the section, I see that after that first breezy exchange about the weather, there's no reason for John to mention the weather again. Instead he'll try to break it gently to Mary that he's leaving. On the other hand, once he's broken the news, Mary needs to talk about the weather more or less uncontrollably, trying to keep him in the room. Her burbling about the sun, the trees, the air will not demand any kind of answer from him so I can't let her run on for too long—just long enough to let the reader know what she is doing, and that she's out of control. Then when John interrupts, trying to say something final, she may talk about the sun on the trees in an attempt to interrupt him, and when he interrupts to tell her it's final, this is the end, maybe she'll say another line or two about the birds or the flowers — just enough to let her tumble into the speech in which she threatens to kill him. All that might arrange itself in these few words:

John: "Mary, I've been looking for you, there's . . ."

Mary: "John, everything is so beautiful, have you looked at the leaves today, they're all gold and the sunlight . . ."

John: "Mary, there's something I have to tell you."

Mary: "I love the fall, the air is always so . . ."

John: "Mary, I'm leaving you. Mary, do you hear me?"

Mary: ". . . so crisp, it makes you glad to be alive . . . alive . . . Yes, I hear you, and if you leave me I'm going to die. No. I'm going to kill you."

Sometimes those characters say too little.

If I know where a scene is going, I'm likely to work too jerkily in a first version, moving my characters from A to B all at once. John comes in and says, "Hi, Mary." She says, "It's a beautiful day." He says, "I'm leaving. Forever." She's on him in a flash, saying, "If you do I'll kill you." The introduction and response are too abrupt in this case. The reader needs time to absorb the scene. If he says hello, she's going to acknowledge him; unless he's braver than I think he is, he's going to lead up to that declaration gradually, and unless she's a fool she's going to try to head him off; once he has the words out she is going to try to pretend he didn't say anything and only after that doesn't work will she make her threat. Once I have drawn the rough version of the scene, knowing the central action and, in this case, reaction, I may have to type and re-type until the conversation moves naturally. Having fleshed it out, I may need to double back to see whether I have said too much. Then I will be relentless about junking every line that does not function.

In writing dialog, I am by no means transmitting speech. I am giving the sense of speech.

You will learn this in the process of writing and refining dialog and not by being told. It is a process which must be repeated with every dialog scene and in time it becomes a natural part of the process; you will do it without even thinking about the fact that you are doing it. You'll know in your bones when and how it is needed. At the same time, I can offer a few suggestions.

1. One test of speech is to read it aloud. If it doesn't sound natural, play it over and over again in your head, altering it until it does. Granted, there are famous writers whose dialog does not resemble human speech; these are writers in full control of their talents, working from a level of experience and sophistication the beginning writer can only guess at. As a writer just beginning to use dialog, you need to discover the truth of speech, listening and refining human cadences. Learn first; later on you can test the boundaries.

2. Once a scene is complete, strike out any line a character says simply

to advance the other character's speech. A character's responses should show something about himself, about what it is like to be where he is just then. If somebody in a play keeps saying "Yes," or "Go on" while another character rambles, the audience catches on quickly. It's not so apparent in short fiction but it's a cheap trick and one to be avoided. If you need to break up a character's speech you can give him a bit of physical business; maybe he's pacing as he talks, or maybe he stops to make himself a drink.

3. Try to keep characters from saying the same thing twice. Often a character will have two speeches so similar that they can be telescoped. This telescoping may cut out the "Yes" Or "Go on" speeches on the part of the other character, giving the scene velocity. Sometimes the characters are saying the same thing in two different ways and one of these exchanges can be cut. This kind of cutting helps shape a scene so that it goes directly from A to B.

Let's say that the hypothetical John and Mary are talking and he says, "The one thing I can't stand about you is your stupid condescending attitude." Then she says something inconsequential, and he says, "You're so damn condescending." Now if he says it once, or even twice for emphasis, it's legitimate, but if she makes some remark and he goes on to say, "I hate being condescended to," then you have to assume he's out of control and so is your scene, especially since her remarks have done nothing to advance the scene. You would certainly cut out his third line; you might cut out his second, leaving the first, and then getting on with the business of the scene. Maybe he says, only, "You're so damn condescending," and she says, "Only because you're such a fool." The scene begins to move.

4. The moving from A to B is usually emotional, often dramatic. Ideally, dialog should function in this way. I was brought up short by a friend who, reading something of mine, pointed out passages in which dialog advanced information and events without enhancing character or atmosphere or the texture of a scene. I learned always to go over dialog to get rid of anything used for purely mechanical reasons. If Mary says, "I have tried to keep busy with my job at the canning factory and my poor invalid mother that I have to do everything for because she has this undiagnosable problem and never lets me go out with men," the line is immediately suspect. John already knows this, and I am trying to use her speech to give information. What Mary would say to John, who knows all this is, "God knows I have tried to keep busy, but there are still those lonely nights . . ." She's dealing with what's wrong with her right then; she's engaged in the business of the scene.

It may help to think of dialog as transaction. People meet and clash or bargain or make or break alliances. The tension between characters is reflected in what they have to say to each other. What they say to each other sets the terms for the transaction. Look for a dialog passage in a piece of fiction by any writer you admire. See if you can take it apart and find out:

1. What each of the characters wants.
2. What is the source of the tension between them.
3. What the progression of the dialog is — what they are like at the beginning and how it differs from their stances at the end.
4. What transaction has taken place here.

If you can establish or determine the distance between the positions of the characters at the opening of a scene and their relative positions at the end, you can begin to understand the nature of the transaction they are making: what the business of the scene is and how the author accomplishes it.

After looking at the work of established writers, examine your own dialog. If, going on to write more scenes, you know ahead of time what kind of business your scene is designed to accomplish — the nature of the transaction your characters are making — you will know better what they are going to say. Everything they say should serve your initial purpose, advancing the transaction, and you need to hone and refine and discard and work on their speeches until the scene does what you want it to.

Writing lines for your characters, you have to think about what goes between the lines. Many beginning writers will go through excruciating contortions to keep from writing the simple attribution: *he said*, or *she said*.

One group will spend two lines identifying two characters and then give you two pages of unattributed dialog and expect you to keep the characters straight. Sometimes it works. More often, the reader is not gripped and moved along, which was the aim; instead he's engaged in the distracting exercise of counting backward line for line to figure out who said which speech. My own rule of thumb is that a reader can always hold six unattributed speeches in his head but somewhere in the next three or four speeches he is going to get lost unless one of the characters is represented by italics or is using a dialect so obscure it is painful to read.

The other group is trapped into writing such lines as: " 'Good morning,' she bustled," or: " 'Good grief,' he expostulated," or: " 'Good night,' she breathed."

There is positively nothing wrong with saying, *he said*, or *she said*. *Said* is more or less neutral and seems to disappear into the reader's perception of a scene without leaving much residue. *He asked* is somewhat more weighted and should be used *only if the character really wants to know*. Characters can also scream, shout, howl, beg, protest, do any one of a number of other things, but all these other words are weighted to some degree and can't be used more than once or twice even in a novel.

Attributions should be organic and they should advance the story in some way, drawing emotional states or physical details that pull the reader into the scene and keep him there. They should complete the prose rhythm rather than interrupt it. In addition to letting the reader know who's talking they should give him time and space to absorb what's going on. A densely packed dramatic transaction may go by the reader too fast. Audiences at plays and movies have the actors' performances to complete the author's intention. Readers absorb words from a page at high speed and they will get *only what you give them*. If that subtle exchange between mother/daughter or lovers or enemies goes by before the reader has a chance to absorb it, the writer's effect is lost.

Here are some rough examples of ways to attribute speech other than the use of *he said/she said*:

Use of addressee's name:	"Shut up, Mary."
Simple direction:	"Duck, you bastard." She threw the glass at him.
	He sighed. "How can you be so stupid?"
Physical description:	She was picking at the fringe on her blue dress. "Because I'm sick of you."
	His face crumpled. "You don't mean it."
	"I damn well do."
Drawing emotional state directly:	He was confused and miserable but he had to find out. "Are you sure you want to leave me?"
Drawing setting:	The sky at her back was black. The clock started ticking backward. "Hell yes I want to leave."
	He said, "Then you might as well know, I was never in love with you."

If you read and analyze enough dialog you will discover that some lines give character or color. Some lines give emotional development. Some give information in subtle ways, while they are doing something else at the same time, and some move the scene dramatically. Testing your own dialog after it has unfolded, you had better kill any line that doesn't function in at least one of these ways.

What remains — functioning fictional dialog — maintains the speed and life of the original, but the original stripped of anything that doesn't belong, streamlined so that it will move swiftly toward the completion of the transaction.

It may be useful for you to name a couple of characters — mother and daughter, for instance, or a pair of lovers or an employee and a bad-tempered foreman. Take any two characters you think you know pretty well and let them *talk to each other*. If you're working on a computer, print out what you have.

First read through, asking yourself:

Questions About Dialog

1. What's the dramatic line I'm trying to draw, and is it clear?
2. What is the nature of the transaction my characters are making?

Then with your answers to these questions in mind, take a pen or highlighter; go through crossing out or enhancing what you have on the page by assessing the speeches line by line, asking yourself the following questions:

1. Is this character's line carrying its own weight or is it just one of those things I've written to get to the part I want to write? Too much of beginning writers' dialog is what they used to call "traveling music"—the hellos and harumphs two characters go through before they get to the point.

2. Has my character said this before?

a. Is the repetition intentional?

b. If it's accidental, can I cut this line and the one that follows?

3. Is this speech explaining something that should have been demonstrated elsewhere in the story? Be careful of dialog you write to *get in background information* instead of *advancing your story*.

4. Does this speech:

a. Sound like the character?

b. Tell the reader something about the character?

c. Advance the scene by establishing or enhancing the tension between my two characters?

d. Say what I want it to? This is a particularly important question if you're dealing in human drama—things changing between two characters. Subtleties may be lost on readers approaching your story from the outside because unlike you, they walk in cold, without a clue as to what's going on.

e. Say too much? You want your readers to know what you have in mind but neither you nor your characters should over-explain.

5. Is this speech:

a. Too short to do the job?

b. Too long for what it does?

Considering the answers to all these questions, making changes to make your dialog tighter and truer to your intentions, you're actively engaged in revising to complete your thinking and in the process, get the most out of the work you've already done.

As you do so, remember:

Functioning fictional dialog is not remembered speech or automatic speech but rather speech abstracted, speech distilled so skillfully that it is more convincing than anything simply remembered or recorded. This is not speech but the *truth* of speech, dramatic and more convincing than the real thing.

9

SHOWING AND TELLING, OR:
HOW TO TELL IF YOUR TURTLE IS DEAD

*E*ither you are in the scene or you are not in the scene.

Either it is happening or it isn't.

Rendering makes the scene spring from the page. The characters come downstage to make their own scenes. The reader sees and hears.

Artful telling has its own kind of life and color and movement. If rendering is bringing the characters downstage, artful telling creates the set and becomes one of the characters, as much a part of the story as the action. In the hands of a skilled artist, the reader will move from passages in which the author shows to passages in which he tells and back again so swiftly that he will not even mark the passing.

Faulty telling is something else. It is narration all on one key and has no art or life or movement. It is a trap for the beginning writer.

Sometimes beginning writers helpless in the face of approaching drama will resort to telling about what happened to a given set of people because they don't have the skill to render the scene. They will tell too much because they can't sort out the right things to tell from the wrong ones. They may tell it because they don't know how to draw a live scene between two characters. They can't write dialog well enough to make it happen. Or they may tell the reader things they forgot to make clear in the earlier part of a story because they've failed to prepare the way for what is to come. They may tell too much because they haven't learned to judge their own work: where the center of this particular story is, what to put in and what to leave out.

How can you as writer know when you are showing, or telling, or telling poorly?

It may help to look at a piece of fiction from the outside and try to make the distinction. Here is part of a scene rendered by George Garrett in his story, "A Record as Long as Your Arm," as told by a narrator caught in bed with his good buddy's wife Geraldine — by Ray, who is until that point his good buddy.

To view you more or less as, say, the center sees the punter on fourth down.

At which point, precisely, you turn back toward the bed, twist, rather; twist your head to look at the bed. Our glances meet. Upside down, of course. And I am happy to see that you are empty-handed.

What else can I do, then, prior to resuming my original position, what can I possibly do but wink?

We're in the middle of the scene, right smack in the middle of the embar-
rassment, with the angry Ray regarding us from the bedroom door.

"Geraldine!" you shout.

Muffled noise from beneath the pillow.

"Where the hell is my fucking gun? I left it in the top drawer."

Ah, a familiar domestic situation. In a trice and a twinkling Geraldine is
back in charge.

"Well," she says clearly and distinctly, "I haven't touched it. Try the
bottom drawer."

Clutching her sheet — in fact all of the sheets pulled out from under me
in one smooth deft yank — she is now rising with every intention, it seems,
of helping you search for the gun.

Wrapped in her cloud of sheets, she is suddenly between us.

And I? Off of that bed in a roll. Scooping up my undershorts like a third
baseman handling a hot grounder. Out the window without wondering if
it's open or not.

Discovering, a good hundred meters away from the house, that indeed it
had been open and all I have wrapped around me is the screen and its
frame. A picture entitled "The Wages of Sin" is moving twinkle-toed,
screen and all, through a series of almost identical backyards in the Whis-
pering Pines Subdivision. Tangling blindly with rows of hedges while trying
to take them like low hurdles. In one case having a memorable encounter
with a portable outdoor grill on wheels. Which sails me along merrily as
far as a blue plastic swimming pool, through which I thrash and splash,
half-drowning, while packs of dogs begin to bark and various lights come
on.

Although the narrator purports to be *telling* all this, we are in the middle
of a scene which is vividly rendered. The author has used a combination of
dialog and action, escalating the language, to make the scene spring to life for
readers. This is what I mean by showing.

Here is an example of artful telling, in which the way the words go brings
the scene to life. Once again we are *there* but in a different way, as Lois Gould
draws the queen's dwarf Morgantina in her novel, *Subject to Change*.

In a secret chamber behind a door in the queen's private chapel, Morgantina sat at a low marble bench grinding her powders, distilling her liquid
perfumes. Bottles stood about, and glass retorts, scales and measures,
pestles and ewers, their contents glimmered darkly in the flickering
candlelight: oils and essences to whiten the royal skin; potions to lighten
the royal mood. It was said that Catherine sent to her native land for these

rare ingredients; it was said that without them her face would be dark as a Moor's, and her humor blacker.

While she worked, the dwarf sipped a sweet liqueur from a tiny goblet made of exquisitely chased gold. This drink she prepared from crushed wings of butterflies, powdered shells of iridescent beetles, nectar of exotic flowers, and a certain flesh. Though she never spoke of it, many believed the elixir to be the potion on which her mother had weaned her, which stunted her limbs and gave her mysterious powers.

The tiny room was always fragrant with this liqueur, and with the essences in her beautiful jars — lime-colored heliotrope, myrtle like liquid sunshine, and, strongest of all, marescialla, an oil the color of burnished bronze, which bore the name of a beautiful marquise burned at the stake in the country of Basques. It was said that as the marquise burned, the scent rose like a bronze cloud from her long white arms, coloring the air of the Pyrenées, lingering over the valleys like a fragrant lament. Years after her death, travelers swore they could tell if a man had passed through the village of Saint Pé, where she was buried; the odor of marescialla clung to his clothes and his body as though a perfumed arm had reached from the grave to caress him.

Yet though Morgantina often spent hours working in this cramped and airless room, she herself never carried the slightest trace of marescialla upon her clothes or her person. It was assumed that the liqueur banished all other elements with which she came in contact. At the same time it would shape her dreams. Often she would doze here, seated at her bench. Yet it was not a true sleep, not a restful slumber. It was the time, some said, when her limbs would extend to normal size, stretching long and shapely as the limbs of a marble goddess. She would feel the stone bench grow colder beneath her body, while her head grew lighter, softer than air. Soon unknown colors danced behind her eyes, in caverns of deep red, in opalescent darkness. Hours would pass, Morgantina knew not how many, but in the end she would behold her own fierce beauty etched in a glass stained with colors of fire. She would grow invisible, yet shining, an aerolith poised upon the crescent moon.

That's artful telling, almost incantation. The rhythms, the use of unusual, distinctive detail and the rich vocabulary bring the scene to life.

Both writers know how to pick a reader up by the ears and put that reader down *in the middle of what's going on.*

A faulty teller might very well reduce these passages to the banal, taking away life, drama, movement, everything except the commonplace. A master simply begins.

As a beginning writer, you need to be aware of how important it is to use everything that comes to hand to make your readers see what you see. It's important to turn everything you know to the process of bringing life and movement to the page, from prose rhythms that pull the reader along to immediacy of dialog, action, language that is distinctively yours and precise choice of detail.

Starting out, you are probably on surer ground *showing* or rendering — dramatizing scenes — than you are telling.

When in doubt, *demonstrate*. Like any angry child trying to get a point across by jumping up and down on a toy, your characters can show readers how they *feel* by what they *say* and *do*. Dialog is action. As Gould demonstrates in the passage above, so is vocabulary. So are prose rhythms. If you work long enough and hard enough you will eventually learn how to use them all. In the meantime you'll want to be particularly alert to the delicate question of whether your story is coming to life.

Readers are always the first to know whether a story is alive or not. Readers also know the difference between showing and telling, and artful and faulty telling. They may not know it in an intellectual way, differentiating as they read, but they know. They know if a piece is static or boring or the author is telling them too much or the wrong things. They know whether they are in the scene or not in the scene, whether they care enough to finish reading, and if they finish, whether they think, *Right*, or only, *So what?* They judge according to effect.

Writers involved in process may think they're doing the one thing when they're actually doing the other. In fact, showing and telling are not easily differentiated. The complicated truth is that writers are telling even when they are showing because the whole thing, whatever it is, is made up out of words. As writer, you may not know, as insider, whether you're showing or telling and if you are telling, whether you're doing it well, so that the telling is an inseparable, functional part of the story, or whether you're doing it poorly, making stacks of lifeless, worthless sentences. In some fiction, the writer finds it easier to differentiate between showing and telling, scenes and non-scenes, because there are distinct differences in manner and technique and each has its place; showing and telling may alternate and be more or less separable. In other kinds of fiction, language and rhythm and velocity combine to make telling showing, so that the two are integral and inseparable; the inner logic of a particular story is so tight and true that everything happening to the writer and, later, the reader, seems inevitable. Readers will not have a moment to stop and wonder how they're being moved; what they *will* know is that they're on their way.

That's all very well, but since all stories present themselves on the page and they are all made out of words, how can the writer as insider tell the difference between showing and telling and faulty telling in his own work?

In kindergarten it's easier. The time set aside each morning is called Show and Tell, and the little kid who has been bragging about his pet turtle or the brass gong Uncle Jack brought from Hong Kong gets to bring in the turtle or the gong and hold it up while he tells about it, pointing to the retractable landing gear on the turtle or the incised design on the gong.

As writer you're expected to demonstrate the pet turtle or the brass gong without benefit of visual aids or gestures, and to make the reader believe in a complete set of complicated actions involving same without ever seeing them, and you have to bring it off using only words. You can use any word or all the words you want in any conceivable combination but as you begin you know you will never have a real live turtle to show the people; you won't even have a picture of the gong.

Instead you have to be quick-witted, crafty and resourceful, using whatever words and techniques work for you, from intimate first-person narrative to omniscient third person, flirting with time, either foreshortening or extending, making the words march or waltz or stagger on command and throwing in anything else that will serve your purpose, from letters or newspaper clippings to little visceral bits of your own, using every trick you know to make the reader know.

I know right now that there is no way for me to give you a foolproof set of instructions for artful telling, because in every case the methods are an intensely intimate part of the accomplished writer's individual makeup, unique to each. This is too closely interwoven with individual talent and process and metabolic style to be separated and examined, and it is determined anew each time a given writer sits down to write a given story.

Instead I can make up simple examples to try to get at some of the ways of showing. There are probably almost as many ways of showing, or rendering, as there are writers, but I have brought a very small turtle with me today and if we look at him it may help.

This would be telling:

The boy came in and told his mother he was tired of chopping wood and she told him he had to do it anyway so they had a fight.

Rather dull. Let's look at ways to *demonstrate*.

Rendering in dialog might be the most direct way of bringing this to life.

"Okay, Ma, I've had it. You can chop your own damn wood from now on."

"If you don't get back out there, Harry, I'm going to kill you."

"You couldn't kill me with a machine gun if I helped you load it."

"Don't be fresh."

"Or maybe you would like me to go and get the hatchet?"

"I'm warning you, don't be fresh. When your father comes home I'm going to tell him you were fresh and he'll teach you not to be fresh."

"I suppose he's going to kill me too."

"I wish he would."

The difference between telling about and rendering action is slightly more complex. For example:

The boy was tired from chopping wood. He came in the room and sat down in the chair.

Versus:

"I split about a cord of wood today." Andy crossed the room in an unsteady zig-zag and fell into a chair.

The only trouble is that there's nothing really wrong with the first example. In the second the boy has a name and we know what he sounds and looks like, so it may be more immediate, but the first might function perfectly well in a certain kind of story.

Maybe, then, the difference shows up more strongly over the long haul. If the author told us that the boy was tired from chopping wood and came in the room and sat down in the chair, and then this same author followed his beginning with more deadpan description in the same tone, we as readers would begin to get restless. What if the writer went on from that beginning to say:

He had a fight with his mother and then he went to bed and had a bad dream. He was always having fights with his mother and bad dreams afterward. So in the morning he got up and killed her with the hatchet.

My own response to this information delivered this way is: So what?

I for one want to see and hear the fight, and I wouldn't mind knowing about those dreams. I want some intimation of what the boy is thinking, if only through his actions, and I want to know how the mother treats him, and I don't want to be told any of these things. I want to know because the author knows.

An author who doesn't want to give me the story through simple dialog or dialog-and-action or action alone can engage me by telling the whole story in the third person, but from the boy's point of view, with those feelings for the mother, those dreams, or from the mother's point of view.

If none of those methods seems right for the material, he can engage me by using internal monolog. Here is one superficial but feasible rendering, in which the boy speaks:

Damn Mom, all this wood, stacks and stacks of it and she doesn't even need it, all she wants is the sound of the ax and me working, and all my bones aching afterwards. She knows that and I know it too, but if I go in there and try and tell her she will get mad at me all over again and I will wish I was back out here chopping wood.

Or the boy can do a straight narration:
I told her I was sick of chopping wood but she sent me back out there anyway, me with a two-bit hatchet and a pile of logs a mile high, I was hurting by that time, I hurt all over, and I thought if she wasn't going to let me quit I was going to have to find some other way to get out of it.

Or the mother could tell the story:
I could hear him out there chopping away, stupid little bastard, why can't he tell I hate him, I thought: If he comes back in here one more time and starts to whining, I am going to scream.

Although the second two examples are ostensibly straight narration, there is an element of internal monolog in both. In the course of telling what happened, the narrators are also letting us know how they feel.

In all these cases the story is happening, so that we begin to see it happen instead of being told about it.

With visual rendering, we move into an area which may be, rather, artful telling. In any case the scene has its own life, and if we, as writers, cannot always distinguish between showing or rendering and artful telling, we can at least know whether what we are writing is alive or dead, and so I will say, rather, that the visual technique, bringing the reader into the scene through external or physical details, is another way of bringing a story to life.

This visual technique can be approached through so many routes that it would be hard to catalog them all. One way would be to describe the farmhouse, the yard, the corner of the yard, the boy, dusty and sweaty by the time the story opens, still chopping.

The farm was located in one of the remote corners of the county, a place where nobody came. The house was not by the road but at the dead center of the property, surrounded by fields and connected to the rest of the world by an overgrown drive. In the farmyard, nothing seemed to be moving except for the boy, who lifted the hatchet over the wood he was splitting and brought it down again, lifted it and brought it down. His face was without expression but the knuckles on the handle were white and he hit each log violently, as if he wished it were something else he was attacking.

The approach is more or less cinematic: we begin with an aerial shot of the countryside, with the farm; we zoom in on the farmhouse and then cut to a long shot of the boy, chopping wood; then we dolly in and cut to a couple of close shots of his face, his hands, the logs, and then pull back for a full shot. In the process, we may or may not see the sleight of hand: although pretending to stick to external details, the writer has assumed something about the boy's state of mind.

Another visual approach would be cutting back and forth from the boy with the hatchet to the mother inside the house, giving physical details to indicate their respective states of mind, using completely external means to bring them to their terrible mutual moment. Still another would be to take the point of view of the absent father or the townspeople discovering the crime: the woman dead and the boy missing; readers will come upon the body when the outsiders do, and then, with the witnesses, they will try to uncover the terrible truth. The movement is the method: unfolding a series of tightly wrapped petals to expose the truth, or horror, at the center of the paper flower.

As I list the possibilities for putting the reader inside a story, actually present at all the scenes, I discover my own strong bias both as a writer and as reader; I want to be there, I want to show and be shown. I want both artful telling, hypnotic as an incantation, and flesh-and-blood scenes rendered, with people stepping downstage to deliver their lines with intimacy and force, but if I have to sacrifice one or the other, I would rather read or write a story with all the action strongly rendered than a story in which none of the scenes are rendered, no matter how beautifully it is told. Most living, breathing stories are a combination of both.

What's become clear to me in a series of discussions with beginning writers is the need in most cases to do more than describe what's going on in a story. As creator of a world you're trying to bring readers into, you may know everything that's going on, and you may have been telling them at length. What you need to understand if you're going to keep anybody's attention in this age of telecommunication is the need to *demonstrate*.

Don't let your characters languish moodily in a nebulous state of mind. Put them into action. Teachers who are inclined to jargon will talk about a troublemaker as "acting out" his problems. Clearly a bop on a playmate's head is more expressive than a good long think about how unhappy the character is.

A writer friend describing her son's girlfriend, who had begun an affair with a new boyfriend in the apartment they were sharing, said: "She did it to get his attention."

Now, looking at your own work, ask yourself:

1. What is my character *doing* to express inner states?
2. Is there enough action to get the other characters' attention?

3. Is there enough to get the reader's attention?
4. Is there a transaction taking place here?
5. Does what I have on the page make this transaction clear to the reader?
   a. By telling?
   b. Or by showing?
6. What can I do to enhance what I have on the page? Can I:
   a. Tighten or compress what I have to heighten drama?
   b. Intensify the action?

Remember, stay flexible. Nothing you write is carved in stone. Be willing to develop your story further through creative revision.

If there is another way to get at the criteria for a living, breathing story, it may be through a series of negatives. Let's look at that turtle I brought to class. If that turtle isn't breathing, or twitching, or doing something else to attract attention, that turtle is probably dead.

Here are some ways to tell if a turtle is dead.

1. If it isn't moving. For example: the boy cuts wood and then he goes into the house and then he comes back out and cuts more wood and then maybe he goes to the store or he kills his mother, but you tell this in the same way you did the wood-chopping, without drama or emphasis, nobody speaks and nothing raises this from dead-level telling into fictional being.

2. If it moved a while ago but you forgot to show us. Maybe you brought the turtle in for Show and Tell but lost track of it because you got interested in the basket you brought it in and started telling us about it instead. The turtle crawled under a bookcase and died of neglect, but you didn't notice until it began to smell. Now you have dragged it out and are trying to interest the class, but nobody wants to hear about a dead turtle. Example: the story is really about the boy's mother and her nervous breakdown. We are following her story with some interest when you remember the boy and break things off to tell us about him. "Listen, everybody, I forgot to tell you about the boy." Forget it. You're too late. Tell us some more about the mother. Now if that boy is out there chopping wood while the mother is inside the house, breaking furniture and screaming for help, *that's* another matter. On the other hand, you should have let us see him somewhere early in the story so we'd recognize him when his moment came.

3. You brought your turtle in, but this was the day you were supposed to bring the gong. The turtle has better sense than you and has pulled in his head and legs; he might as well be dead because he doesn't belong. Example: the story is really about the sheriff and his partner, whizzing by in the car. Although the boy is part of the scenery, he has no other significance. The lengthy description of the boy chopping wood has no place in the story at all.

4. If nobody cares whether your turtle is moving, the turtle is dead. This is a subtle matter of engagement. The writer must be engaged with his characters and the story he is telling or he will have a hard time engaging the reader. We are willing to watch the boy chopping wood up to a point, but the scene has to belong to the story, by virtue of its function in the story, and we have to move on from that scene into some kind of action or conflict or that story is as dead as any turtle.

5. If it is smothered in detail. You brought in your turtle, but you had him at the bottom of a box of pages from your coloring book. You were really proud of the coloring and couldn't bear to let it pass unnoticed, but nobody in the class cared enough for those pages to lift them all out and uncover the turtle. Example: We see the boy in the farmyard chopping wood and we hear all about the kind of wood he is chopping and the way he does it and there is too much attention paid to the brand name and cut and fabric of his work clothes and the maker of the boots he is wearing, or where he went the last time he had them on, and then we hear all about the hatchet he is using and none of these details point in any particular direction; the author is telling us so much that we stop listening.

6. If you brought your turtle in because you wanted to talk about the message you have painted on his back. It doesn't matter how noble that message is, even if it's: Everybody should love everybody, or, We should put an end to war. We know, we know. A story may carry any number of microdots or messages by implication, but the primary function of fiction is not to teach, it is to make the reader believe, and too much explicit intellectual or moral freight is going to squash it. If the only reason for launching a story is to deliver a message, then the story is the wrong vehicle. Example: the boy cutting wood is meant to be the living embodiment of the downtrodden laborer everywhere, exemplifying the plight of the underpaid worker, and his mother is the capitalist boss personified. What you want to show is the evils of capitalism. Or the whole thing is a Freudian paradigm. There had better be something more going on in that story, something coming directly out of the characters, who they are, what's the matter, what they *want*, or it is as dead as any turtle.

Now, about that turtle I brought to class. I put him down somewhere a minute ago and he seems to have wandered off. Before he left I think I heard him say, "If you want to send a message, call Western Union."

He must have heard what happened to those turtles in the pet department down at Woolworth's, the ones with the peace symbols and the American flags painted on their backs. They all died because somebody put too much paint on their shells.

10

Detail, Symbolism?

*E*very word you pick up is loaded.

As a result I find it depressing to talk about symbolism. I don't think the word belongs in the working writer's vocabulary — so long as the writer's still working. You may know about it as a reader or as a critic but when you sit down to write fiction you had better set it aside. Symbolism is something to be talked about from the outside, by outsiders, after the fact.

Granted, symbolism delights critics and keeps them busy long after the writer has gone on to other things ("And what precisely is the significance of the whale?" or: "What did she mean by *that*?"). At the same time it can cripple beginning writers, who may undertake work with an overwhelming sense of obligation to certain literary conventions, so preoccupied with Paradox and Deeper Meaning as commodities to be obtained somewhere outside the work, ahead of time, and shoveled into the work, that they will overlook their own specific and extremely individual sets of emblems.

As writers we may begin with the apparent meanings of words — the dictionary defintions — and a sense of the generally accepted significance of the objects which surround us. All of us move from this into our own private and specific sets of meanings. We will never misuse a word, in the technical sense, any more than we will mistake a chair for a dog or a tree, but by the time these things have passed into our heads they have picked up additional freight in the form of strongly personal meanings.

I think this happens to everybody all the time.

One of my sons revisiting an old summer camp said, "I'm going to see the mother." He was talking about a cabin and an association he made when he was five. The Kiddy Campers called the counsellors at that camp "mothers." On the first day of camp, somebody said, "Look, there's the mother." Being absent-minded, this particular son of mine looked the wrong way and fixed on a rustic building with wide porches and no glass in the windows. It pops into his mind, whole, every time somebody mentions the word "mother."

For me, the word "grizzled" will always call up the image of my high school geometry teacher. Her name was Eloise Boozer and she alternated the brown gabardine dress and the green gabardine dress and powdered her face like a busy postmaster cancelling stamps. When somebody says "farm" I play a whole medley of remembered farms, and sometimes the word "woman" brings

WOMAN in block capital letters and at other times the Botticelli Venus.

If you say, under your breath, "mother," or "grizzled," or "farm" or "woman" you will see something completely different from what I see, or what my absent-minded son sees, or what anybody else sees. If we talk about Duluth and none of us has ever been there, we will each have our own vision of Duluth anyway — and it won't look much like the real Duluth.

Writing, I can never make you see precisely what I see, but by using care in the selection of the details I choose to give you, I can make you see some of it. If I work with enough care, I can make you see beyond your individual vision to give you some sense of mine.

With this in mind, I hate to talk about larger, internationally recognized symbols such as ocean = mother or tree = life or bird = freedom or even the man in your short story as representative of art and the woman as symbolic of life. It is also why I don't want to talk about symbolism. I think it is an outsider's word that abstracts and limits something which is potentially extremely rich and intensely personal.

I think it is foolish and wasteful to try to intellectualize a basically visceral process. All writers have storehouses of emblems, and these emblems have distinctive meanings. Part of the process of writing is learning to recognize them and draw on them.

As a writer, I can look back *after the fact* and pick up certain themes in my work, certain preoccupations. If I write about being asleep as like being under water, it is no coincidence, nor is one particular recurring element: the missing father. There is a lot of food served up in my fiction, from Napoleons in a moment of high festivity to the frozen tuna pot pie eaten by a character in despair, and in retrospect, this seems significant. So do the telephone calls; people miss connections in my fiction. Interesting, I suppose, but this was not what I was thinking about in the heat of the moment. Writing, I was thinking about *what it was like to be those people in that place at that time*, and I was ready to use everything I had to create the scene and put the reader in it. In each instance I was writing at the level of happening, because each scene had to have life. If there is more there now, it is because a given scene had life in it.

If there is symbolism in any of my work I'd rather not hear about it because as an insider, I don't want that kind of outsider's judgment of the work. My fiction has to emerge from within, developing naturally, and my primary concern as writer is who the people are, what's the matter, what they *want*. If one of my characters happens to be serving time chained to a pole at the apex of a steel cone for the edification of a global television audience, I am going to be diffident about the suggestion that either the pole or the cone has sexual significance. At the time I wrote about it I was thinking only of what it would be like for that person: what he felt like, struggling for purchase on the slick sides of that cone; how uncomfortable it was to be chained to a pole. If I am belligerent about this, it is because I am convinced that story comes first, it has to come first, and if somebody wants to take symbolic meaning from it after it's finished that's their business, not mine. As the man said after he'd finished the first wheel and rolled it off into the bushes: I invented it, now any damn fool can play around with it. I will come out into the open now, with a frank admission. Writing fiction, I am in part trying to understand and order life, from the inside, instead of grasping for some external set of meanings and trying to apply them.

With this in mind, I will always fight shy of symbolism.

I prefer to deal in terms of detail.

Look at these three passages.

From *St. Urbain's Horseman*, by Mordecai Richler:

Mrs. Hersh, an early riser, usually lay in wait in her bedroom until she heard the children in the hall, a grizzly old hen perched on the edge of her bed, her flat brown eyes melancholy. So this morning, typically, when Nancy started downstairs with the baby in her arms at seven thirty, followed by Molly, followed by Sammy, Mrs. Hersh opened her door to join them. Mrs. Hersh was wearing pink flowery pajamas and slippers with baby-blue pompoms. The winged tips of her glasses were silver-speckled.

We know Mrs. Hersh. She has life. We know what she looks like and we know quite a bit about her from what she's wearing. She doesn't have much taste; the pajamas tell us. So do the glasses. Now I am ready to admit that the Mrs. Hersh that Mordecai Richler wrote is not precisely the Mrs. Hersh I see, because as reader I have projected my own set of meanings, which are probably close to the ones he drew from, but will not be identical. I see her as one of those wonderful lower middle-class Jewish women who will refer to her friends as "girls" and pass her time at club meetings with the girls, lunch parties with the girls, bridge games with the girls. You will not see precisely what Richler drew or even what I saw, but what you see will flower into life from the details he has given you.

Hortense Calisher treats the *nouveau riche* in her novel *Eagle Eye*:

What he could never hear fully was what they were yearning for, comfortable as they all were, and getting more so. Everything they wanted seemed to be flowing toward them. In his father's office, ever larger on each state visit, lines of desks were starred with faces Bunty didn't know any more, or who didn't know him. At home, sofas overflowing with pillows, the beds changed for posture ones, and pictures of a kind he had never seen before on his home walls. What was this yearning that went always a little ahead?

We see the family's rise reflected in the increasing size of the father's office, in those lush sofas, the expensive posture beds. Because these are more general details than Richler's, we'll build the sets inside our heads. Calisher hasn't even named the artists who painted those pictures but we know they represent the Newest Thing — whatever the newest thing happens to be in the year we read the book. Although they are less closely defined than Richler's, it is the details which bring the passage to life.

We go on to look at Bunty's parents:

Now they had it, now they didn't; they had some of it, would they get all of it? — their faces said to him as they stood there. Maeve the redhead, with her narrow bones, fine skin and freckled hands whose large joints she complained of, was three inches taller. To Bunt, already taller than both, his father now looked endearingly small and solid, his face cherub-nice, not cherub-nasty — a teacher had taught him the difference. "The nicest smart man I ever met," one of the desks had confided. "Is he ever gonna get places. You watch."

At once we have a sense of them. Because, unlike office furniture and posh apartments, people are going to look more or less the same in any year, Calisher is more specific about their looks. Whether or not physique determines character in real life, it often indicates it in fiction, and so we may think of her as neurotic, him sunny; the story is on its way.

John Cheever describes a house in *Bullet Park*:

Nailles's house (white) was one of those rectilinear Dutch Colonials with a pair of columns at the door and an interior layout so seldom varied that one could, standing in the hallway with its curved staircase, correctly guess the disposition of every stick of furniture and almost every utility from the double bed in the northeast master's room through the bar in the pantry to the washing machine in the laundry basement. Nailles was met in the hall by an old red setter named Tessie whom he had trained and hunted with for twelve years. Tessie was getting deaf and now, whenever the screen door slammed, she would mistake this for the report of a gun and trot out onto the lawn, ready to retrieve a bird or rabbit. Tessie's muzzle, her pubic hair and her footpads had turned white and it was difficult for her to climb stairs. In the evening, when he went to bed, Nailles would give her a boost. She sometimes cried out in pain. The cries were piteous and senile and the only such cries (or the first such cries) the house had heard since Nailles had bought the place.

I'm there. I know the house. I recognize the dog. They spring up before me — not precisely the same thing Cheever saw, but what he has given me superimposed on my own set of images, fairly closely defined in this case because he has been extremely precise. I have seen such houses; I've seen dogs like that. I already know a great deal about Nailles from his house and the way he treats his dog.

Without playing Laocoön, strung up in a tangle of critical trappings, I'd like to suggest that in each of these passages the objects named and details used have meanings beyond their superficial ones, that in one way or another they signify something more and deeper than the surface value of the nouns, and that we don't really need to belabor or examine that fact any further, but only to understand that, reading, we will assume some of those same meanings and that the details have given the fiction life.

Writing fiction of your own, you will not go headlong into a minute catalog of the trees on a given street or the color and size and shape of every piece of furniture in a given room. Instead you will give readers a sense of being there — sometimes through selected details, sometimes through one or two impressions. You will let them know what *kind* of a street it is, whether they're going down an asphalt street in a shady, well-to-do suburb or walking barefoot down an oyster-shell beach road in Florida. It means indicating the sidewalk, *if the sidewalk is important*, and only a writer's instinct can tell you whether it is. It means picking out the given object or set of objects, the sideboard or the collection of jade or even the pattern of light on the floor, which tells most nearly, most exactly *what it is like in a given room at a given time.* You will do this by deciding what's important to you.

Imagine a room. If you can't make the leap, then write about a room you remember.

Writing, you know what it's like in that room because you are there. Being a certain character in a given room, you know what's there and how much he will see — which things he will think are important. If you are furnishing that room with objects dredged up from your own specific compound of memory and imagination, that alluvial sludge, they will be the right ones, complete and real. What's more, whether or not you see beyond the room as you create it, these objects will already be fully fleshed in your own individual set of meanings. They carry a certain freight of their own — what they mean to you as well as what they will mean to the reader beyond the meaning you intended. Your characters will develop significance in that same intensely personal context: you know who they are as you become them, and discover what they want; in turn they carry more significance than you thought you had given them. If they are whole and real they will take on life in the reader's mind and this life will have its own meaning — yours superimposed on what the reader brings to it. In some wonderful and real way, supplying external details is often the best way to get across the more complex, internal ones.

Let me show you how you can make details work for you.

To be specific, we'll start with the weather. What is it like in a given place on a given day? We all change with the weather to some extent, whether we fall into fits and rages in deep August or succumb to the February slump. Your character may find himself faintly hopeful in early spring, watching the first crocuses fighting their way through light snow, or he may only be distracted by a light breeze which ruffles his hair and takes his mind off something he was about to say. Sometimes his moods will work counter to the weather: he'll glower at a bright Saturday morning, obscuring the sky with black thoughts; maybe he'll look into a spring landscape and imagine the flowers wilting and the trees withering under his murderous eyes.

Writing about detail, I understand that I can't separate detail from character or from the story. The details make and define the scene for me as writer, and as they do so they are yet another reinforcing element of inner logic. I am not only furnishing the rooms in a given story; the details I choose will affect the story, working on the characters even as I select them. They will both affect and indicate the character's inner states.

In this context everything becomes important, from physical surroundings to physique to costume to mannerisms and speech. I will never give all of this to the reader, but I need to know it all as I work: where the characters are, what they look like, what they're wearing, how they talk and what they're doing as they speak.

To begin: What is the place like? If this is a room, is it large or small, cluttered or nearly empty, unique or characterless? Is it easy for people to talk here? How do they move in the room? How does this particular character respond to the room? Visiting a woman friend, is he enraged by expensive, impractical silk upholstery and gold-framed mirrors that cost enough to keep a family of five in groceries for a year? Maybe he's going to be depressed because this woman whom he admires so much lives in a dump in a welter of papers and books, with no more than an unmade bed, a rusting desk lamp, a broken chair. His response will be conditioned by the fact that people's rooms often tell a great deal about them: what they think is important, what kind of objects they choose to surround themselves with, how they take care of them. As I give the room and the character's response to it, then, I am also telling you about the owner of the room. Again, the details I choose are working on both the character and the reader.

If I hear a character and become him, I need to know what it feels like to be inside that body, which means that I have some idea what the person looks like. I may not find it necessary to give the reader more than one or two details, but I must know.

Incidentally, what is he wearing? Clothes may not make the man, but like surroundings, they can indicate a great deal about him. Elia Kazan once said people dress according to their expectations; that's part of the picture. They also dress according to what they think of themselves—whether they think they're beautiful or ugly or insignificant or important, and if they have one of those hale and hearty self-images psychiatrists like to promote, their costumes are still going to be determined by what they think they are doing that particular day. Are they wearing work clothes because they are really working or want to fade into the woodwork as just folks or are they trying to gross out pretentious parents, or has the man slipped into a Russian raccoon coat and the woman into a simple little drop-dead dress?

There is a marked difference between the man who clings to his old tweed jacket with the English vents and the man who wears Italian suits and highly polished boots. There is even a difference between the man whose tweed jacket with the English vents is old, soft, comfortably worn, and the man whose jacket is stiff, brand-new. Between the woman in black leather and the one in black silk. We have advance opinions about people who wear hardhats or leisure suits; the man who wears a wide tie with a palm tree painted on it is not the same man as the one who wears an understated tie from an expensive men's shop, and a writer who writes as if there were no differences misses a great opportunity.

Mannerisms—from tooth-sucking to hair-twiddling to eyebrow-smoothing to knee-jogging—give a character individuality at the same time as they indicate inner states. When a character is upset, or frightened, or pleased, these mannerisms may disappear—or they may be intensified. They take on added value as another character responds to them. A character's flustered gesture can tell the reader more about him than any number of explanatory sentences. The infinite range and variety of creation are evident when we look at *people*; no two people are alike and there is no reason why two characters in fiction should be. A character may be completely described down to his socks and still remain a cipher because he has not been set into motion. Conversely, he may stick in the memory because of mannerisms, even though the writer's physical description has been sketchy.

There is, finally, speech, a complex and changing thing which varies from region to region, from class to class, from moment to moment and from character to character. If you as writer are alert and listening, replaying those tapes in your head, you will have understood and abstracted for yourself the cadences of certain *kinds* of speakers—your characters. Let me say only that details, as I describe them here, can reinforce speech.

A character may bellow into the heat of late summer or speak softly into a wind. He may talk while turning a paperweight or a bit of amber over in his hands and put the object down just as he makes his point. He may bring himself to say something difficult as he picks his way through a crowded room.

As he talks, his aspect may change. He may bloat with anger or shrink in humiliation as he stammers out an apology. He may pull at his tie or draw his coat around himself, or he may roll up his sleeves and open his collar in an attempt to be one of the boys.

Whatever he does as he talks will indicate his mood and sometimes his motives in a perfectly human, understandable way.

By talking about all this I don't mean that I think every moment of every story has to come out in living color and with stereophonic sound. The best writers do not go on and on relentlessly, filling in every single little detail without any attempt to select or shape. Instead they will know all the details, and give the reader only what is needed. We'll talk about selection at length in the next chapter.

As you work, furnishing the empty rooms of fiction from your own storehouse, you will pick and choose in an individual way, basing your decisions not on academic concepts of symbol as significant ingredients supplied from somewhere outside the story, but using precisely what you need to make a story work for you. All your choices, from larger concerns like character and action and setting to use of detail will be determined by the composition of your particular deposit of alluvial sludge and the inner logic of the specific story you are making; both of these will inform and be informed by the nature of your own particular vision and the nature of your own specific compulsion to tell. If you are sensitive to all these sources and work directly from them, your work will have strength and meaning which gives it life precisely because it is uniquely yours.

You are already too rich to use symbols (let's shift to a bass voice and bark a little louder: SYMBOLS) as objects or units of meaning to be conceived intellectually and imposed from the outside.

Every word you pick up is already loaded.

Let it be.

Questions About Detail

Rereading your story for detail, ask yourself: *What makes this person/room/ object/setting different from all others?*

1. Do I have a clear picture in my mind of what this person/room/object/ setting looks like?
   a. From memory?
   b. From imagination?
2. Have I described it accurately?
3. Is there anything I've forgotten that I need to supply to make the reader see what I see?

4. Have I provided enough detail to make the reader see what I see?
5. If not, is there anything I can add?
6. Or have I supplied too much? Instead of *selecting carefully*, have I taken the lazy way out and put down every single detail I can think of?
7. If so, can I identify the most striking things about this person/room/object/ setting?
8. Which details are most important to me?
9. Which are most important to the story?
10. With the answers to these questions in mind, which details about this person/room/object/setting can I eliminate to highlight the rest?

11

WHAT TO LEAVE OUT
AND WHAT TO PUT IN

*I*t's easier to talk about what to leave out of a short story than what to put in.

You leave out everything that doesn't belong.

The inner logic of a given story will determine this to a large extent. Each choice you make will focus and channel your work. Everything: the words you choose, ideas, characters, belong in a particular story *only as they function in that story* and you as writer are going to have to be ruthless about getting rid of anything that doesn't belong.

Short fiction is particularly demanding. Novelists are permitted occasional indulgences because the stage they occupy may be as intimate as a theater-in-the-round or large enough to accommodate a cast of thousands including elephants, but a writer of short stories has a relative space the approximate size of a puppet stage. If you let things get out of control you will end up knocking over scenery and threatening the entire arrangement with collapse.

The business of a short story of three to ten thousand words must be accomplished in such a limited compass that any misstep can throw the entire story out of proportion. At every point you need to resist the temptations to digression: falling in love with the sound of your own voice, or following a lesser character for too long because she happens to be interesting. If she is that interesting, either the story is focused in the wrong place or else the character is pushing you into something larger, a novella or a novel. If the landscape takes over, then maybe the story is about the landscape and not the people in the foreground; in either case the story is out of control and you are going to have to make sacrifices to bring it into focus.

If you are working with some concern for inner logic, you'll discover before long that most of the major problems solve themselves. Given a specific set of choices, or givens, you have already excluded a great many things, beginning with anything that disrupts the mood. A comic story may be a number of things besides funny, and almost anything can happen, but it had better be told in a way that maintains the reader's sense of comedy, and a story which is essentially serious in tone will go haywire if you try to tack on a funny ending unless you have prepared for it. If you're going to throw a custard pie at the end, you'd better have it behind your back the whole time.

Given a certain point of view and a specific place to stand, you've already excluded other kinds of points of view and places to stand. Given a set of characters, you know by their nature which kinds of things they will do and which they won't, and which of these actions belong in the story. Each defining choice will strengthen your sense of what belongs and what doesn't.

The simple rule of thumb is: *everything you put in a story had better function in the story.* If it doesn't function it doesn't belong.

Beyond the built-in understanding supplied by inner logic, you may find some use for a simple set of rules.

Here are some things to leave out of short stories.

1. What characters do between scenes. If two people have a fight at the office and then they go to their respective homes and have supper and pay the bills or make some phone calls and go to the movies and go back home to their respective beds and get ready for bed and get in bed and go to sleep and wake up and have breakfast and go to the office and meet again and have another fight, it is quite likely that we don't need to know about it. All that extraneous information can be implied by dropping them at the end of the fight:

"All right, dammit, I don't care if I never see you again," and picking them up in the next scene:

Naturally the next morning they saw each other again, as they had every morning; after all, their desks were side by side in the same corner of the office.

If, on the other hand, one of them has gone home and constructed a pistol out of some cotton wadding and gunpowder and length of pipe, we had probably better hear about it.

This is a gross example of an extremely complicated matter: all that eating and sleeping didn't belong in the story, but anything that grew out of the fight, anything that would affect the outcome, did belong. Anything that serves character or development belongs, but the things characters do *between* things can simply be skipped. We as readers are familiar enough with quick cuts and dissolves in the movies to be able to fill in the blanks for ourselves, and, furthermore, to assume with very little prompting that a scene has shifted.

2. Unnecessary dialog must go. Only the important business stays, and although you can hint that people are having a boring discussion about the weather, you had better not give it in full. Another gross example:

"Good morning Mr. Ransom," Higgins said.

"Good morning, Higgins."

"Nice day we're having."

"Yes it is, isn't it, Higgins?"

"Yes, I think so, as a matter of fact it was so lovely out that I walked."

"Did you really?"

"Yes, it only took another ten minutes, and the sun felt so good on my back. Everything is in bloom."

"I know, my dahlias are out already, and Mrs. Ransom is very excited about the marigolds, we're going to have thousands of them this year, but by the way, Higgins."

"Yes, Mr. Ransom."

"You're late."

"I know I'm late sir, but I thought you would understand, you know, how beautiful it was out and all, how lovely the flowers were . . ."

"I love flowers just as much as you do, Higgins, but if it hadn't been the flowers it would have been your car stalled, or you found an injured pussy-cat, you're late today because you're always late and I'm getting damn sick and tired of you being late."

OK. The business of the scene is that Higgins takes his sweet time getting to the office and for Ransom today is the last straw. Unless their fight is going to culminate in Higgins going over and poisoning Ransom's garden, or something that happened on Higgins's walk to the office is going to function in the story later on, all you really need is:

"Good morning, Mr. Ransom," Higgins said. "It was so beautiful out I decided to walk."

"Late again, Higgins."

"The sun was so warm on my back, all the flowers are out . . ."

"Forget the flowers, Higgins, you are late."

We have arrived at the confrontation without any detours.

3. You can leave out anything you had to write to get from one point to another. Sometimes this is a scene which you, as writer, had to work through in order to know what was going to happen next. Sometimes, as in the weather dialog above, it's what you had to make your characters say in order to discover for yourself what the true business of the scene was. If the business is the one man being late and the other man being angry, we as readers might like to know that the one is late because of the weather, but that's all we need to know, and it can be done in a single line. Character descriptions written to help the author discover character, or extensive physical descriptions written to help the author discover setting or action, should be combed relentlessly. Anything that does not enhance the finished story, anything that distracts or bores the reader has to go.

4. You can leave out elapsed time. This is so logical and obvious, the process is so simple that many beginning writers don't see it at first. Faced with a gap of days or weeks or years between one crucial event and another,

they will find themselves writing in summers and snowfalls from a compulsion to *fill the space between events*. Movies and television have educated this generation of readers and writers to the quick cut, the flashback and flash forward, the shock cut and any number of other techniques; we have absorbed them by osmosis and whether we realize it or not, they are a natural part of our equipment. You already know these things; you can put them to use in fiction. IF NOTHING GOES ON BETWEEN ONE SCENE AND ANOTHER, CUT DIRECTLY. Most of us as readers have become so sophisticated about filmmakers' cuts from one scene to another, from one location to another, that we are more than ready to make any leap an author asks. We can be moved from one scene to another, from one location to another so swiftly that we walk into the next moment without stopping to ask how we got there.

5. You can leave out most explanations. You can assume that your reader knows almost as much as you do about your setting, or the occupation of your central character. No reader does, but for complicated reasons which I'll attempt to get at here, they'll blame their own ignorance. There is a mysterious authority to the printed word. One of the most important things you as writer will learn is how to exercise that authority. Readers who don't know everything about offices, or newspaper city rooms or steamfitting or long-distance running seldom blame the writer for not filling them in. Instead they will feel faintly guilty in the face of your assumption that they do know, because in assuming that they know, you are also implying that it is their business to know. What's more, readers will resent you if you assume they're ignorant and slow down a story in order to explain.

If it is important to the story, your readers will find some way to supply the missing details as best they can, and if you, as writer, choose to give a few clues or crumbs of information to head them in the right direction, they will fall on them with gratitude. Depending on who they are, readers will fill in the details in one of three ways:

a. They will put in what you have left out, using their own store of knowledge to create the setting. The newsroom you see may not necessarily be the one they furnished in their minds, but it will function for them. They'll use everything they've read or heard or seen on film or TV to put together a functioning background for your story. They will do the same for a story whether it takes place in an insane asylum or Alaska or the army.

b. Or they will read carefully for context, and figure out the details from what you have given, combining what you give with what they already know to fill in the picture. In *A Clockwork Orange*, Anthony Burgess imposes an entire vocabulary on his readers by the relentless use of new words in familiar contexts. After a few pages readers know that tolchoks are blows and peeting is drinking and they accept an alien vocabulary for the same reason. Burgess doesn't explain; reader doesn't refer to his glossary. Reading swiftly and for context, reader figures it out. The same goes for Ernest Hemingway and his *cojones*.

   c. Or, if readers feel guilty enough about being ignorant, they'll find some way to find out what they don't know. They'll look it up or ask somebody. They'll do this because they know you are assuming they're just as smart as you are and they're moved to live up to your expectations. They will, furthermore, be pathetically grateful for whatever they learn from context and will absorb whatever details you have given into memory banks for use the next time they're faced with a similar problem. Thanks to you, they get wise; the next time they're faced with a newspaper city room or a steamfitting shop or a long-distance race they'll nod sagely. Yup, yup, we know about this one; uh-huh, uh-huh, yeah.

   Here's an example. It would be possible to begin a story about a reporter as follows:
   The city room of an evening newspaper is organized according to function. There is a U-shaped arrangement of desks with the city editor sitting at the center of the U and the rewrite man sitting next to him. On the paper in this story he is responsible for everything that goes into the paper that day; he will decide which stories to send reporters out on and which stories already written are important. He may also make the dummy (showing the composing room which headlines belong on which stories in which size typeface) and mark this on top of the copy before passing it on to the men who sit around him in the U. They are called desk men and they read the copy for errors and write the headlines. The reporters all sit at desks ranged around this central U. They have certain regular assignments, but if anything important happens the city editor will make them drop everything to go out and cover the story. They will telephone the rewrite man with the details and he will put on his headphones and type out the information as fast as it comes in because the deadline is coming and they have to get the story set up in type as quickly as they can so it will be on the front page of the first edition. On an evening paper, the first edition goes to press around noon. Ralph Carlson was a reporter on an evening paper, and he was having his lunch one day when the phone rang and Henderson, the city editor, answered it . . .

   Although all that information is background, there is no real reason to give it. All the writer needs to give is what functions:
   Henderson was in the slot that day and when the first call came he listened for a minute and then turned it over to Casey, who was on rewrite.

Then he bellowed, "Carson, Williams, there's a hell of a fire at Wooster Square. Get on over there."

"Right." Carson dropped his sandwich onto his story about the Fresh Air Fund and left the newsroom on the run.

Henderson was already on the phone to the composing room. "Tell Ray to hold Page One."

The gentle reader who doesn't already know this is a newspaper office will find out quickly and will, furthermore, feel stupid for not catching on sooner. "In the slot" implies a position of responsibility and the reader will figure out that Henderson is an editor and in passing will learn a new phrase. By the end of the story readers will know what the rewrite man does, as the embattled Casey takes in bits of information on the phone and gets the story in shape for Henderson. There is a sense of urgency about ripping up Page One to accommodate this new disaster, and if the sandwich doesn't indicate it's lunchtime, it doesn't much matter. Any real insider will know it's accurate. Meanwhile we as readers are being treated like insiders. By the time the story is over we'll have a pretty good idea what newspaper work is like without ever being instructed. We are involved because the writer assumes we are on the inside of what's going on; even though we may not know exactly where the writer has put us, we're grateful for being considered smart enough to be along on the trip. What's more, we're learning all the time.

Remember that readers hate being condescended to. We all like to think we've been around, and if you insist on explaining at length we will resent that, and, strangely, we will begin to question your authority. Who is this writer trying to convince? Is it really us, or is it himself? Look for the right details to put your reader in the picture and do it with authority. Never apologize for knowing more than your reader does, and never stop to explain.

6. Leave out loving descriptions unless they function. You can give the reader a room, a landscape, any kind of a setting, using as wide a sweep of prose as the subject commands, but you do so only if this room, or landscape, or setting, or object is going to function in the story. That ormolu clock on the mantel in the old man's sitting room may be a marvel of workmanship, but unless you are going to use it to signify time passing or as an emblem of the grandeur of the old man's past or his regrets, or unless somebody is going to come in and brain him with it, there is no need to describe it in detail. That autumn landscape that so takes your imagination is suspect too. No matter how beautifully you describe it, it must assert its function in the story in order to belong. You may use it as background, or as the first frame in a sequence that will narrow down to a certain piece of property, the house on the property, a given room in the house, the people in the room. You may set it against the

moods of the people in the story or use it in any number of other ways, but if it is there simply because you liked the way you wrote about it, you are going to need to be ruthless. Beautiful as it is, it is going to have to go. Otherwise it is going to stand between the reader and the story like a misplaced flat in an amateur theatrical.

Deciding what to leave out, you will test everything you put in, discarding everything that does not belong. Once you have finished a story you will need to go back and look again, paring, amputating if necessary, until everything that is in the story serves the story.

Once you have developed a relatively sure sense of what to leave out of a short story, you have yet another responsibility: deciding how much to put in. Short stories written by beginners are often sketchy at best, and a new writer dealing in subtleties may assume that because the writer knows what is going on, the reader is going to know too. Such writers may respond with surprise or resentment when the story fails to come across, saying huffily that it's the reader's fault if readers don't get it.

This is not necessarily the case.

Writing, you need to put in enough to make a functioning story. You may be as sensitive and subtle as you like, but, working, you must be clear in your own mind about what you are attempting. You need to know what is the center of your story, and you have to be able to focus, to give the reader enough information so that the people you are trying to reach will know it, too.

This is subtle and complex territory. Attempting to write short fiction, you have to supply the indefinable and elusive element which distinguishes story from non-story, and if there is any way to learn about it from the outside it is by reading short stories by the hundreds with some attempt to understand what the writer is doing to you as reader, and how. Having done so, you will still have to write stories by the dozens, perhaps even by the hundreds until you as insider feel the movement, the extraordinary number of possibilities for different kinds of movements, and understand at least one of them well enough to convey it to the reader.

I have suggested that as writer, you are already rich in resources, that every word, object, name, action or reaction or speech or stylistic device you choose shapes what you are doing, and that in addition to its more or less universal associations and meanings, each of these has accumulated accretions in the alluvial sludge at the back of your mind, so that every element takes on added value as you use it *according to what it means to you*. If you are good at what you are doing readers will take all these enriched elements, perhaps enriching them further with their own emotional baggage but at the same time receiving what you intended to give.

It is here that you must take the most care.

You have to put in enough for the reader to go on.

Using your intensely personal store of references, you can be as subtle or experimental or ambiguous as you like, but there had better be something there to reward close scrutiny and it had better be precisely what you intended. If your meaning is private you can't take it for granted that a good reader is necessarily going to get it, and you'd better not be angry with careful readers if they don't. It's probably your fault.

Within the framework of what you are doing, there has to be that focus, that consistency of intention or meaning that a close reading will reveal to the reader who is scrupulous enough to track it down. If the careful reader doesn't get it, don't be too quick to blame; look at the work again and be at least as quick to question your own judgment as you are to question others. If your reader couldn't figure out what you meant, could it be in part because you weren't precisely sure? Or were you sure, but careless or imprecise in the way you gave it? Obscurity coming out of authorial uncertainty and imprecision is just as damaging to short stories as a monkey wrench thrown into the electric fan.

There is no easy way to talk about this.

Our friend the electrical engineer introduced me to the information theory, which was developed during a study of military cables transmitted during World War II. Since he used to talk about analog computers with a condescending aside ("giant electronic brains to you"), I have to assume that his explanation was simplistic, and there is also the possibility that I got it wrong. What I extracted has been useful to me and so I offer it here.

As I understand it, the good folks with the computers were engaged in discovering just exactly what percent of a given message had to be transmitted for the intent of the message to get through. If wartime cables were too garbled in transmission, if too many parts were left out, the whole intent was lost. Either the message was misconstrued or it didn't get through. If a certain crucial percentage of the message was presented, the mind would supply whatever was missing and the message would go through.

The writer needs to supply enough to give the reader the meaning the writer intends. This can be done with great subtlety; the reader is capable of supplying enormous amounts, doing a large part of the work, and so sharing in the excitement of discovery. On the other hand, as writer, you want readers to make the discovery you intended them to make. You don't want them to invent some wild story loosely based on the sparse elements you have given. The delicate balance, then, is to give enough to carry your readers through to your intended meaning, or moment of discovery, without having to spell it out word for word.

This means that although your readers are going to supply whatever is missing, they are going to supply a wrong meaning unless you give them enough details or information to point them in the right direction. If you write a story without a center, readers are going to try and find one; after all, they have trusted you this far, and because they trusted you enough to come this far with you, they have to assume you brought them here to some purpose. If they emerge from your story without discovering the center, they still assume you are telling them all this for some reason and unless they've already given up in disgust, they will supply one. Nine times out of ten, you as writer aren't going to like the construction outsiders put on your story, and whether or not readers give up on the meaning or supply a wrong meaning, your work is wasted.

This means that it is extremely important for you, as writer, to know what you are trying to do in a story; where you pick the reader up and where you want to leave that reader at the end. Then it is your business to put in *enough* detail, or action, or information or a combination of all those to reward the close reader and prevent gross misinterpretation.

You must write like an insider, because you have to be an insider to write. Having done so, you need to re-read like an outsider, and adjust accordingly.

Questions About What to Leave Out and What to Put In

By this time you should have a draft of your first story in hand. Read it, trying to identify for yourself *all the items that truly function in the story*: scenes, descriptions, details. Try to sort out the things that belong and separate the ones that don't belong. *Now that you know how your story comes out*, ask yourself:

About What to Leave Out

1. Does this story begin at the beginning? If not, where does it begin?
2. How many paragraphs or pages have I written just to find out where it starts? What can I eliminate?
3. How about the language? Can I pare down or tighten the sentences to make them more powerful and precise?
4. How much space have I given to *transition*: what people do on their way from one scene to another? How much can I eliminate?
5. How much description have I written because I liked the way it sounded? How much can I trim or eliminate to focus my reader's attention on the real business of the story?
6. In supplying detail, have I piled up so much that no specific detail has much importance? Which details are most important? Can I get rid of the rest?
7. How many lines have my characters said on the way to what they really

mean to say? Which ones can I cut to emphasize what's important to my story?

8. Have I tried to use two scenes where one would do? Which stays and which goes?

Next, look at your story, and *now that you know how it comes out*, look at it carefully to be certain all the elements are there. You want to give enough information to supply your meaning to your reader. It's time to ask yourself:

About What to Put In

1. Is everything clear here, even to an outsider?
2. Is my dialog in each scene complete?
3. Do I need to add a few lines of dialog to make clear what's going on between my characters?
4. Are my readers going to know what's important about my story, or do I need to add scenes or enhance dialog to underscore my point?
5. Am I being too subtle here, i.e. have I taken my readers' powers of understanding for granted? Without over-explaining, what can I supply to make the picture complete?
6. Have I done enough to *show* my readers what's going on, or have I only *told* them? Do I need to *demonstrate* by adding a scene?

Asking these questions, you want to be willing to go back to your story and trim here, expand there, working until what you have in your head lines up with what's on the page. Now it's time for the next step.

12

AUDIENCE

*D*eciding what to leave out of a story and what to put in, you've faced the fact that you're not alone. There's somebody out there. Without looking up or stopping work to count the house or do an ingratiating buck and wing, you have acknowledged the audience. Now it's important to go on working as if you haven't seen them.

You have to resist the temptation to put on slap shoes and a fright wig and win their hearts with a little song. You need to turn your back on them for the time being and get on with what you are doing. If you try to anticipate them, what they want, what's going to make them stand up and cheer and garland you with praise and money, you're dead before you start.

Audiences are a messy group at best, amorphous, intransigent, hard to identify, and if you set out to write what you think *they* want, writing for a particular market or magazine or along lines you think are chic right now, your fiction is going to fall flat because it expresses your own faulty idea of *them*, what *they* want, and nothing of you. Because you can never know *them*, only yourself, the fiction isn't going to be true to them and it won't be true to you either. Without the life of conviction, fiction dies on its feet.

Most writers I know harbor occasional secret dreams of selling out and making a lot of money. Wouldn't it be wonderful to spend a few months on a shlock best-seller and then live the rest of your life on the proceeds? I used to think if I could just master the *Ladies' Home Journal* formula I could knock off, say, two *Journal* short stories a year at $2500 each and worry less about money. I would, of course, spend the rest of my time on my serious, double quotes, "serious" work.

As I set out to do so I discovered what hundreds of other writers already knew. If you are a serious writer making a cynical attempt to do something cheap for quick money, it's all over before you start. No matter how careful you are, some of that gravity or care for the work will creep in; it won't be enough to redeem the work, just enough to dilute that racy commercialism, turning the work into a hybrid unfit for the marketplace.

It didn't take me long to learn that you can't make a sow's ear out of something else. Trying, you run the danger of traducing or losing that something else. My stories written "for money" were never going to make money. They weren't even good stories. They were bad by any standards. I was never going to write glorious trash that pleases millions.

I think, furthermore, that if you're going to write a shlock bestseller, you can only succeed because you believe in what you're doing, and for no other reason. If you follow newspaper interviews of the money-making popular writers, the showbiz stars of the best-seller list, you will discover that they are completely serious about what they are doing. One writer I know tried to separate his careers: he wrote successful trash under a pseudonym and reserved his real name for his "art." His trash made a lot of money, it was *good* trash, and I would have congratulated him on his success at that which the rest of us only dream of, except for the fact that his "art" wasn't much good and besides, he was getting defensive about his trash. He felt compelled to write about it in a national magazine, murmuring about Balzac and defending his trash as the best thing in American realism since the works of Theodore Dreiser.

To make good fiction at any level, you have to believe in what you are doing. Works written for a specific market will almost always fall short because you have abandoned your own inner vision for a faulty, externally imposed set of rules: the standards of a certain magazine, or what you imagine to be the standards of a certain magazine. As a writer, you have to work according to your own lights, making each story as good as you can make it *in its own terms*. When you're finished working from the inside, when the story seems complete, then you can stand back and look at it from the outside to find out where you might sell it.

If you write with your eyes cut to the left, counting the house or trying to anticipate the audience, if you fail in concentration because you're already listening for applause, the work will fail too. You will lose your audience before you even know them. Self-conscious performance can never be total performance. Unless you give your attention, your hopes and your best efforts to the work itself, the work is going to fail.

If the audience is out there but we're not supposed to play to them or even acknowledge them until the work is finished, what good are they?

I think readers serve two functions.

First, they will let you know whether you have done that which you set out to do. They may also help you cover the distance between what you have done and what you thought you were doing. This response covers the range between the friend or teacher who reads a first draft and doesn't get it and the publisher's editor who reads your novel and doesn't get it and presses you to explain.

Second, they complete the work by being there to recognize it. Without getting into larger questions of Life and Art, I'd like to suggest that the things we make to please ourselves — stories, paintings, even costumes — are in one sense like Bishop Berkeley's tree in the quad. They may exist even if nobody sees, because we have fulfilled one part of the urge, expression, but our works will have only a partial existence, ghosts in a barren landscape. It takes audience to complete them.

I refuse to believe that the world is filled with mute, inglorious Miltons. Quality surfaces. If you are writing, and you care enough to keep writing through what may be months or years of rejections, chances are you will find your audience. It may be the readers of a "little" magazine instead of *The New Yorker* or you may find yourself writing novels that reach only a few thousand readers instead of the runaway bestseller, but if you are good enough at what you are doing or are willing to keep on working until you are good enough, you will find somebody out there who recognizes you, who understands what you are trying to do and acknowledges that you have done it well.

This finding of audience level is interesting. I have said that I believe our stories and books are in us from the beginning; without sounding fatalistic I'd like to suggest that writing from the inside, trying to make each piece of work as good as possible *in its own terms*, we are like water finding its own level. A writer I know said, "When writers go on making small sales year after year, they're likely to blame their agents or their publishers or this review or that one and think if they just changed that, they could be famous. I think it's us, and what we're writing. I know only certain kinds of people want to read what I want to write about."

Being true to what you have to say, you will find your own level. If you're not true to it, you may not find any audience at all.

My guess is that if there were no audience, most of us would not be writing. Dictating my first book to my mother at five, I wanted her and my father to admire it. Drawing the pictures to go with it, I remember knowing the phrase, "illustrated by the author." By the time I was twelve I found it necessary to send two books "illustrated by the author" to a children's publisher. I also remember knowing ahead of time that when Sister sent me from the seventh grade up to the ninth grade to read my composition, the ninth graders were going to hate me for it. I didn't really care because I liked the idea of having a room full of people listening to me read what I had written. The response, some external proof that what I was writing was better than average, fueled the desire to write.

We may think first of audience as something necessary to the completion of the work. It takes longer for us to recognize that we can use readers as reflectors. They can tell us when we have accomplished what we have set out to do — and when and how we have fallen short.

Giving somebody else a piece of fiction to read is a touchy matter at best. Feelings are involved. If the response is negative we are likely to blame the person instead of the work. More than once I chalked up a teacher's objections to obtuseness or insensitivity and stalked away. It took years for me to understand that I was right to refuse to take specific suggestions about what to do to a story, but I was wrong in assuming that all the fault lay with the reader.

If the reader didn't love it, chances were there was a problem. It was the critic's function to tell me something was wrong. It was mine to figure out what to do about it. Over several years, showing my fiction to my resident critic as soon as it rolled out of the typewriter, I learned how to use this immediate audience as a reflector.

He might say, "I like it but there's something the matter."

I would become defensive. "What do you mean, there's something the matter? Show me."

"I can't show you what's the matter, I only know something's the matter."

"Then show me where."

"I can't."

I would be getting huffy. "If there's something the matter why don't you tell me what to do about it?"

"You're the writer."

"If you can't tell me where it is or what to do about it, there's nothing the matter." I would clutch that day's pages defensively and go back to my desk. Once I had recovered from my spell I was able to think about what I had learned from the encounter. If a piece hadn't gotten the response I'd hoped for then it wasn't accomplishing what I thought it was, *in that version.* I was going to have to keep working until it did what I wanted it to do.

I suspect this is the major function of criticism, whether in an editorial conference or a class or a reading by a close friend. A good critical reader does not prescribe or find solutions — but can offer a diagnosis.

It is in this area that, as writer in the process, you can best use an audience. Most beginning writers nurse the secret suspicion that what they have just done is perfect. If you have just finished a story that you are convinced is just right, and four out of five readers say there is something the matter, then chances are there is something the matter. They may try to identify the problem and if they do, they probably won't agree on where it is or how you should solve it. Somewhere between the intention and the act, in the process, your work has fallen short and the best these readers can do is let you know this. Now it is up to you to figure out precisely what to do about it.

As you sit down to analyze responses, keep two things in mind:

1. You're trying to go the distance between what you're trying to do and what you have here on the page. Look at your reader responses and see:

   a. Which comments are useful.

   b. Whether everything you thought was clear is clear to your first readers.

   c. If not, what you can do to make it clearer.

2. Now, and this is most important, *discard everything that isn't immedi-*

ately useful. Having admitted that nothing you write is perfect the first time around, you can be equally sure that no reader is a perfect critic. Writers survive and triumph by deciding which criticism is useful to them and which isn't — and discarding anything that isn't going to help them.

Take your readers' response for what it is, a sign of trouble, and retire gracefully to try and work it out.

The less time spent blaming the readers, the better. The audience has fulfilled its function as reflector and trying a wider audience, or a different audience is not going to change the nature of what you have on the page. No matter how many readers you approach, you are going to find that they are all saying the same thing. An editor of mine has a wonderful way of locating responsibility. She says, "It's not all there yet," or, "It's partway there," or, at a later stage, "It's almost there." Only when it's all there will she be satisfied. She has made it plain that if the work is not all there then the rest of it is still somewhere inside me and only I can bring it out.

Assuming that a problem exists, you know the solution must come from inside you. You can't simply add this or graft on that according to suggestions supplied by well-meaning outsiders, because anything inserted from the outside is going to affect your work in some of the same ways a wrench thrown into a whirring fan can destroy it. Admitting there is a problem, and that they have pointed it out for you, you can thank your readers and furlough them. Now you need to identify the problem for yourself in your own terms, and work and rework until you have found your own solutions.

Dealing with audience is particularly painful in this early stage, whether you are writing on your own or discovering yourself as a writer in a classroom. Alone with our work, most of us are inclined to think it's quite wonderful. Beginning to show work to others is a little like being brought up unexpectedly to a mirror. Is *that* what I look like? Gosh, I thought I was prettier.

I think getting used to readers' responses at this early stage is important because it helps make the writer tougher, less vulnerable to hurt feelings and more receptive. Unless you as writer are satisfied to stay at the secret diary stage for the rest of your life, this combination of toughness and receptivity is going to figure in your relationship to your work and to other people for as long as you go on writing.

If you're just starting out, and are feeling brave enough to start showing your work, you may need some suggestions as to where and how to find readers.

If you're still in school at any level, there may be classes available in fiction writing. If not, you can probably show work to a teacher or to a classmate you trust, or to friends or family.

Resources available to any writer include family, friends, roommates or housemates. If you know other people who are writing, you may be able to get together to share work for informal discussion. At the formal level, most communities offer adult classes for people who want to write; community colleges and colleges with extension services usually place ads listing classes available, so keep an eye on the newspapers. If you can't immediately locate a class, try telephoning the nearest college or university. Whether or not you want to spring for tuition in an official writing workshop, the faculty may be able to put you in touch with other people in the area who are writing.

Another possible way to find an audience and put yourself in touch with other people who want to write is by going to a summer writers' conference. Most advertise in the book review sections of Sunday papers and in periodicals directed at people interested in writing. Most also send brochures to the English departments of colleges and universities. Nobody learns to write in the few days available to people who attend, but you'll have an opportunity to meet professional writers and editors who staff these conferences and at most, you'll get a manuscript conference — criticism by somebody who's being paid to give your work close attention.

Seeking outside readers, you need to understand that not everybody is going to applaud and tell you you're wonderful. And you need to teach yourself not to feel bad about it.

Anybody who wants to be read outside the home or the classroom will be dealing with criticism for a lifetime — from publishers' readers, from editors, and in time, perhaps from reviewers. It takes fibre to be able to accept what comes with good will and maintain the strength to go ahead in spite of weeks or even years of negative responses. It takes conviction to be able to go on doing what you are doing, and it takes a certain kind of intelligence to be able to extract the best from the criticisms offered and make use of it — and to discard the rest. You will not compromise in order to reach an audience but you will understand that unless you are willing to go the extra mile in terms of listening and writing and rewriting and if necessary doing it all over again, you are never going to reach them.

Questions About Audience

Looking for reader responses to your work, ask yourself:

1. Where do I want this story to leave this reader, i.e. what am I trying to do here?
2. Has this reader responded the way I expected?
3. If not, did I show this story to get applause or do I really want to identify problems?
4. If my readers identify problems, am I willing to listen to the criticism?
5. Can I find ways to use this criticism:

     a. To identify problems in my work?

     b. To find ways to solve them?

6. If I don't like what I hear, is there somebody I can turn to for a second opinion?

7. If my readers agree that there is a problem, am I willing to go back to work to try to solve it?

8. What can I do to close the distance between my intentions and my reader responses?

9. Can I remember to solve my story problems in my own terms instead of expecting my readers to give me ready-made solutions?

10. Am I willing to rewrite and come back for another reading?

13

STYLE

*N*ovelist Paul Horgan says literary style is metabolic, as much a part of the writer as his adrenalin level or his pulse rate, and I think he is right. If you read aloud from a collection of short stories by recognized writers, you'll find that nobody's work sounds like anybody else's. Look at the page and you'll see the words don't even arrange themselves in the same way; blocks of type and white space take on a distinctive look according to who's writing. A writer's style is strongly personal and individual, stamped in brain and bones and nervous system; it emerges and defines itself as that writer works, and it reflects and expresses the writer in profound ways which are inseparable from the content of the work.

It may take you as beginning writer years to discover your own style; some never do, but I believe it is potentially there from the beginning. I think style begins in the ear. It's what it sounds like inside your head, and that is an amalgam of everything you've read and the ways you think and the language you speak and hear spoken. In part, it will be informed by the kind of fiction you choose to write, whether it is comic or dramatic or philosophical or psychological, and I should say here that these choices are never accidental. I think they are determined by who you are and whatever it was that made you want to write in the first place. They are implicit, as much a part of you as the sounds in your head. Underlying these influences is a basic set of rhythms which will determine the ways you write about that which you have chosen to write about.

Your own style is not necessarily the first thing you come to, or the first that comes to you.

The first style a new writer comes to is usually the easiest, and it's likely to be somebody else's. Most of us begin by reading the kind of thing we would most like to write, and end by writing the kind of thing we would most like to read. Beginning to write, we discover that it comes easily. Only later do we understand why. Usually some powerful writer whose works we most admire has moved into our head bag and baggage. Those are his cadences echoing, his choices asserting themselves on the page.

Novelist Walter Van Tilburg Clark traced influences among student writers back in the 1950s. Most of them began with a Fitzgerald period and moved on into Hemingway, or started as Hemingways and became Fitzgeralds. The next period was usually a Faulkner period, which was followed by a Henry James period. Usually James was the last influence; from that elevation, the writer could launch himself, trying the wings of his own newly discovered style. More recent easy influences would include Salinger and Barthelme and Mr. Vonnegut Junior, Anne Beattie and even Jay McInerney. It's perfectly all right to imitate that which you admire, up to a point. Sooner or later you have to understand that this is only imitation, and move on.

Once we have emerged as grownups and writers, most of us are relatively strong, but I would have to confess that I have avoided reading James because I suspect he is powerful enough to be dangerous; I'm going to save him for my old age. I have one novelist friend who refused to read any fiction at all when he was working. He was scared to death he was going to catch something. I think he has a point. Even now if I read a writer who is strong enough, I'll walk away from the book muttering in those same cadences. As soon as I get some fresh air the feeling passes, but I didn't used to recover quite so fast.

The first things I wrote sounded like the first things I read; they all began, "Once upon a time." By the time I was eight my style had verged into early comic book with hints of L. Frank Baum and I slid from there into something which was the product of all the sea stories and horse stories I had ever read, with an inescapable overlay of melodramatic voiceover straight out of the media: "The city sleeps. Over it, in the darkness, a great hand flexes and begins to move . . ."

I didn't write much in high school, but by that time great chunks of my experience were translating themselves into narration anyway. I was hearing things at least half the time; I couldn't help it. At the moment, I can't sort out the sources. Some of them had to be Edna Ferber, which the Beaufort High School library had in quantity, but this was crossed with fiction from the women's magazines, which we read in the library during study halls, and which specialized in heavy romance and light household comedy. I would have to factor in novels in every house we ever visited and assorted selections from the Book-of-the-Month Club during the three years my parents belonged, beginning when I was eight. I read whatever fell into the house and tried to re-create it.

No wonder I was hearing things. I would be at a beach party and during lapses in the action I would hear myself describing myself: "She sat on the end of the breakwater alone, looking over the silvery path on the water, into the cool, blue moon. Behind her on the beach the others played, forgetting her." On trips I would try out lines, usually last lines. I remember one, written for a woman in an insane asylum: "You see, I like it here." For reasons which elude me, that was the whole point of that great unwritten story.

By the time I reached college we were all writing like J.D. Salinger and we all sounded like Holden Caulfield most of the time; we all said "great" a lot, and worried about who was a phony and who was not, and short stories had to be told in the first person because that was the only way to do it because after all, you know?

That phase lasted longer than it should have. While other people were going around writing like Fitzgerald or Henry James, I was going around writing like J.D. Salinger. As I recall there were two sets of theme music playing in my head, one the background music from *Catcher in the Rye* and the other a series of trills and organ strings which accompanied third-person narration that would have done credit to the writers of *Inner Sanctum* or *The Shadow*. Fitzgerald and Orwell and Evelyn Waugh may have elevated it slightly, but the tone was still pure CBS, or was it MGM?

Maybe it was in the course of five years as a reporter that I started sounding like myself. I couldn't imitate fiction because I wasn't writing fiction. There wasn't any point in modeling my news or feature stories after anybody else's and so I just wrote. The reading I did during that period went into my head and merged with everything else instead of bubbling up right away, unchanged. By the time I did get back to writing fiction, my work sounded like my own. Not even *The Alexandria Quartet* could come between us.

I think the experience freed me to some large extent from the influences of all that reading. I was listening more closely to the sounds inside my head: rhythms and cadences, speech patterns which were there before I ever learned to read.

As writer you learn from everything you read and everybody you talk to, but the cadences come directly from your own speech, whether it is American English or the Queen's English, and if you are an American your English may have its roots in regional, black, Jewish, rural or urban American English.

I don't mean we all end up writing the slang we used as kids. We don't write our books in dialect either. I mean simply that our own rhythms and patterns, the way we put our words and sentences together, the placement of rushes and pauses all tell the world precisely who we are and where we come from.

Your own style, when it surfaces, will have its roots in what you hear at home, and this has to do with national origins, cultural levels and something so quirky that I can only call it personal style; families have unique ways of talking among themselves, and whether we like it or not, most of us carry echoes of our parents. After all, where did we learn to talk?

My parents were Southern but their grandparents came from the North to South Carolina and then moved on to Florida. Because I lived in the South for a while I can do certain Southern things in prose when I want to, but because I never lived anywhere for long, my prose is not particularly regional. Still it is distinctly American, mine, and I am especially sensitive to it because I know I am suggestible.

When I am in Beaufort, S.C., I say "Hey," instead of "Hi," and I am not above saying "might could" instead of "might be able" and "Y'all" seems natural. When I am in England I speak a species of what I think is the Queen's English, which at the time convinces me, even though it will never convince my English friends, and I find the Queen's English is so powerful and pervasive that I know I have to go home before I begin to write poor imitations of what I hear. Although I can change color in conversation I know that when I get back to my typewriter I had better be that same American person, so I will not stay anywhere else for too long because I'm afraid of losing my ear.

I worked too hard, listened for too long, wrote for too many years discovering my own style to want to jeopardize it.

The rhythms are there for all of us, innate, informed by everything we say and hear and enhanced by our reading, but discovering them, developing and securing them for all time demands a lifetime of hard work.

I think you will begin to discover your own style when you understand what it means to write a sentence more than once. Guided by correct definitions and the rules of grammar, you will know how to write a correct sentence, but this is only the beginning. Within the range of correct grammar and accepted definitions there are dozens, perhaps hundreds of ways to say what you want to say. The inner logic of the given story, your rhythms and intentions will all help you to determine, for instance, which modifier you are going to apply to a word like "water" *in each particular case.* Is water the right word? Do you mean ocean or lake or sea or fountain or what? If it is a fountain is it sparkling, rushing, spitting, sprinkling, drizzling, rushing in great gouts or dribbling in a pathetic flow or trickling off to nothing or has it gone dry?

These are choices you have to make for yourself: the right word under a given set of circumstances. Whatever the sentence, you will need to write it more than once to discover both what you are going to say and how you are going to say it. Refining the language, you will discover the value of precision, because you are also forging ideas. This is what I mean when I say "once more through the typewriter."

If you care enough to work through borrowed styles and mannerisms, you will discover your own prose style. It is already potentially there. It flashes in and out of your work right from the beginning. Trying to identify it and take hold is another matter. In the beginning it's a little like trying to catch Bambi, and if you are not very careful you may end up with only a few tufts of fur, or, worse yet, a handful of Faulkner and Hemingway.

Reading can help you discover your own style *only if you read enough.* This means looking at fiction by so many writers writing in so many different ways that you will not be seduced by the tone or cadences of any particular one of them. No matter how widely you read, you are not going to discover your style until you have completed the process by beginning to write.

Finally, you will only find out what you sound like by continuing to write and rewrite until you find the right way *for you* to say what you are saying. You bring all your natural equipment to this process along with everything you have learned by reading other writers. If you write and go on writing for long enough you will begin to hear what you are writing. If you listen carefully your own rhythms will assert themselves and help direct you. If you care enough about what you are doing you will go on writing beyond influences and affectation until your prose sounds like nobody else's.

Even though there are no rules, I can give a few cautions.

1. Mannerisms are not style. In college I went through a period of omitting "the"s, and with a number of my friends, perhaps under the heavy influence of Joyce and Gerard Manley Hopkins, succumbed to coining hyphenated words. Some time around our junior year we made up a last hyphenated word to describe the process: saffron-splintered, and then we quit. Maybe I owe a debt to Holden Caulfield after all; what we were doing was phony.

2. Bad grammar isn't style either. Readers find it hard to believe in a writer who gets things wrong. If he's intent on wrenching the language or using it incorrectly, how can they believe what he is saying? If you are unsure about usage in a particular case, look it up in Fowler or Strunk and White.

3. Finding new meanings for words may enhance your style, but making up new meanings for words will not. The wrong word is still the wrong word no matter what noble intentions you have for it, and nothing you can say or do is going to make it right. You can use a single word intending more than one meaning, but all the meanings you intend for it have to be right meanings or you will end up with nothing. If you are trying something dangerous, check the dictionary.

4. If a piece of work comes too quickly, be suspicious of it. Walk around it a few times and then stand back for a careful look. It may indeed be the product of a natural burst of inspiration, but it is also possible that the reason the prose came so fast was because it wasn't yours.

5. Watch out for clichés. Other people have used them with such frequency that their value is already diminished. You need to treat everything you write as new, and this means finding new ways to say what you mean.

6. Watch out for old familiar phrases: phrases familiar to you. You may notice that the people in your stories are always listening with excitement, or speaking dejectedly, with shoulders slumped. Your own pet phrases are going to be so individual that I can't pick them out and warn you. I can only say watch out for this kind of repetition—phrases you have used so many times

that they become as valueless as clichés. Every writer has to avoid self-parody.

7. Test for frequency of use. Except for strictly functional nouns and verbs and articles, few words can bear much repetition. Some are troublesome if they turn up more than once on a page; others can be used only once even in a novel. "Magnificent" strikes me as the kind of word which can be used about once every three novels, if then; "blazing" is another. Words like "nacreous," "arcane," "vivid" and "enormous" all occupy a certain amount of space and need a lot of space around them. Because every word you use bears its own freight plus the freight you bring to it, you have to be careful about frequency. Any word you use too often will lose its value and cease to work for you. If you work on a computer, *Find* will locate your repetitions.

8. Cut out every word that doesn't function. If you have written: "He was most certainly depressed by what he saw," you will change it to: "He was depressed by what he saw." You may even cut it to: "He was depressed," since you have already told us or are about to tell us what he sees that is so depressing. Again, this is an individual process which you must learn firsthand. A good rule of thumb for cutting is to avoid qualifying or reinforcing words like "very," "certainly," "really" when used in the sense of "very." They will usually dilute what you have to say. Again, your excesses will be different from my excesses and you will have to learn this process on the job.

9. It's a good idea to avoid slang except in dialog, and you had better be suspicious of it even there. Slang gets moldy faster than week-old bread and the next time you go back to your prose you may discover that it sounds as silly as this middle-aged friend of mine who goes around saying "hubba hubba" because it was up-to-the-minute about fifty years ago.

10. Watch out for colorful writing. A great many grammar school teachers with the best possible motives have at least temporarily corrupted the style of a great many students by insisting on adjectives applied to every noun and adverbs used in large quantities and outré nouns or verbs in places where much simpler words would have been more effective. More is not always more. In student work, it is often a great deal less. Restraint is important. If a woman turns up at a party wearing a dress with too many bows and ruffles and sequins and too much jewelry and a few too many ribbons and ornaments in her hair we may be so put off by what she has on that we don't care to get close enough to find out who she really is.

11. I think idiom does have a place in writing, but each writer has to test his own idiom according to personal intentions for a specific work and then judge it according to the rule of frequency. I think idiom is a living, breathing part of dialog and first-person narration, but beyond those points the writer needs to develop a strong sense of where it does and does not belong.

12. It may be a personal quirk, but I think unless a word is already in

your vocabulary and it got there naturally, you have no business using it. We all learn new words every day, and once they belong to us they are ours forever. Using them, we will use them correctly. If that right word for the right thing is at the tip of your fingers and you can't quite remember it, or if you remember it and are not certain you're using it right, by all means look it up, but forget about the thesaurus as a stepping stone to fresh expression. I had a friend in college who wrote saffron-splintered poetry with the aid of a thesaurus. Her poems were pretty, but about as individual and expressive as a Sno-cone: colored syrup on crushed ice, with no substance and very little flavor. We never found out what she sounded like because the words she used weren't really hers.

This all sounds more complicated than it is. I think you will learn to refine your prose as soon as you understand that the first choice is not necessarily the right choice, and if you care enough to write, eventually you will care enough about writing to want to find the right way to do it.

Questions About Style

Reading your own work, ask yourself, *What does the prose in this piece sound like to me?*:

1. Does what I have on the page accurately reflect what I hear inside my head? Has the rhythm established itself? If not, are there:
   a. Cuts I need to make?
   b. Things I need to add?
   c. Sentences that need breaking up to establish the rhythm?
2. Am I saying what I mean here?
   a. Is this the right word?
   b. If I'm not certain, does the dictionary say I'm right or wrong here?
   c. Can I choose a more distinctive word from my own working vocabulary?
3. Are my intentions clear to the reader or do I need to add adjectives, adverbs or phrases that will make my work more precise?
4. Is my work so overloaded with adverbs and qualifying phrases that my reader is going to bog down in it?
5. Does this word or phrase sound familiar?
   a. Because I use it too often?
   b. Because it's a *cliché* that's been overused by too many other writers?
6. Have I used too many words to do the job? What can I cut away to make my story more effective?
7. Can I strengthen my prose by cutting out repetitions?
8. Does what I've just written sound like my own work, or do I sound more

like some writer I've just read, or my favorite writer?

9. Have I been honest in my choices, or does what I've just written sound *too* special because I'm substituting mannerisms for style?

14

OFFICE PROCEDURES, OR: SYSTEMS, ROUTINES, THE SECURITY CORNER AND ALL THE THINGS YOU DO TO KEEP FROM GOING CRAZY

*I*f you are going to be serious about writing fiction, there is some practical advice I can offer.

Inspiration may flicker in and out among the tall pines of your imagination like a spotted deer, but the greater part of writing fiction is hard work and, like most hard work, it is better done according to some kind of schedule. This means attempting to do the same things at the same times every week, if possible in the same place. It makes more sense than you think, and for a number of reasons.

Although the more sensitive and freedom-minded of you may blanch at the very idea of a timetable applied to what is ostensibly an art, I can report firsthand that a schedule is one of the most liberating schemes a writer can think up for herself.

I have friends who work all the time. If you drop in on a weeknight or a weekend they are working; if you drop in during the work day they are working; one went so far as to have a typewriter stationed on his coffee table when he was giving a party. The guests would discover him feverishly putting the final touches on the third act as they came in. Blushing with the fine flush of creation, he would whisk the whole thing away and start mixing martinis. I should add at this point that few of the people I know who work this way ever get anything finished. There seems to be something inhibiting about working all the time because there are no times when they are consciously *not* working. Instead they go around in uncomfortable states of mingled guilt and frustration because they never have any free time since they won't quit until they finish and they never finish because they can't quit. They never get away from the work long enough to renew energy and see it in perspective.

There are a few writers who work in bursts, and others who can work anywhere, any time; at least one novel I know of was written in part on our front steps on a Sunday afternoon in November. Some people can manage this. I don't think there are many.

Most writers I know keep office hours. This isn't as rigid as it sounds. It only means that if the appointed hour comes and the writer isn't at his desk, he is consciously *not* working; that this is when he usually works. Furthermore, when the appointed hour comes and he is at the desk, the force of habit is so strong that sooner or later the work will come to him, even if he sat down with a mind as empty as an artificial pond. One of the evangelists of the Forties advised everybody to assume "the attitude of gratitude." If you *look* as if you are waiting to receive the light, sooner or later the light is going to come.

There is more to it than that. Working on a regular schedule means that there are dozens of times every week when you don't have to work because you aren't supposed to be working. In a strange way, it expands free time. I don't work except on weekday mornings, which means that I'm not allowed to work in the afternoons or after supper and I'm not allowed to work on weekends because that isn't when I work. What a relief: I know I don't have to think about it, and I don't feel guilty.

The additional bonus is a gathering of momentum, a storing up of ideas for the actual time spent at the desk. I make myself stop before I go stale, and when I get back to whatever it was I was in the middle of doing, that I remember as going so well, I look at it with a fresh eye and return to it with enthusiasm. I even look forward to working. Problems which seemed enormous on Friday may have solved themselves in the subconscious by Monday; even if they have not, I am rested and ready to go at them.

The weird thing is that this kind of schedule cuts through procrastination. It yields more free hours than it takes away. One of my friends who used to work all the time went to a psychiatrist and discovered, several months and a couple of thousand dollars later, that all those years when he couldn't spare any time for fun because he was working, he wasn't really working. Instead he was fretting over working, putting off working, feeling guilty about not working, and the reason he couldn't come out and play was because he hadn't accomplished anything. The actual work always took place under enormous pressure in the last feverish hours before a deadline. Now he has more freedom.

At a certain level, of course, a writer is working all the time. I have hundreds of notes to myself on everything from old envelopes to theater programs and church bulletins and the paper wrappers from Lipton's tea bags. Entire speeches or long periodic sentences may present themselves while I am looking attentive at somebody's lecture or stuffing clothes into a washing machine. They stay in note form until the next work morning.

This is one aspect of a slightly more sophisticated operation: concentration. A writer engaged in a work of any length is engaged in it at every level until it is finished; it sits in the consciousness waiting to be realized. The writer who knows this is also aware that what goes on between the hours spent at the typewriter is important, whether it's reading or working out or shopping or sleeping. Most writers find it impossible to work on more than one piece of fiction at a time because it fragments concentration. Many writers can't teach and write at the same time because both teaching and writing use the same kinds of energy and it's bad for concentration. Student writers who are also actors find concentration disturbed if they are cast in a play while they are working on a piece of fiction. They need to give everything to either one pursuit or the other.

If you want to write and write seriously you need to be able to give all your creative energy to it. Once you have committed yourself, you can make the schedule work for you at a new level. The time away from the desk becomes as important as the time you spend at it.

As writer working on a scene, you may find it presents itself in vestigial form all at once on the first morning. The next day you're likely to discover that what you thought was all there needs to be developed more fully; perhaps the lines are there but all the other elements, from external details to emotional undercurrents are not clear. A third morning of work reveals a whole series of new values in the same scene. In the time you have spent away from the desk, the work has developed and expanded.

If you stage your work over several days instead of writing at white heat for seven or eight hours straight and calling it finished, you will find that what you are doing gets both richer and denser. You won't write at any greater length but what you do write will be fully realized. I urge student writers to set a regular work schedule — even if it's only an hour a day. After they've done this for a few weeks they understand that all that free time that falls between hours spent at the desk is working for them.

The schedule is only part of the operation. Another part is the security corner. It may seem idiosyncratic to anybody who hasn't tried it, but this is yet another aid to concentration. Most writers have an office or a corner of one room where they can go to write and leave their books and papers placed exactly as they want them without having to stow the whole mess because somebody is coming to visit. Anybody who insists on working in a central place where other people come and everything is going to have to be moved for lunch, dinner or company, is creating a self-perpetuating excuse for never writing anything. Most writers are snappish about privacy and learn to approximate the security corner wherever they go: the light here, the pad or typewriter here, the copy holder there, re-creating the necessary circumstances with any old lamp, anybody's table, even a borrowed typewriter in any old corner, as long as it is a private corner.

Most writers also have preferences, which range from the mild to the pathological, for kinds of papers, typewriter versus pen or pencil and yellow sheets versus notebooks versus the kind of paper that provides its own carbon. If they travel, they will approximate these materials.

I think all this order serves two functions.

For me at least, the external order is important because it is one of the defenses the inhabitants of the twentieth century can establish to keep from going crazy. If we are shoring up bits of typing paper and cotton ribbons instead of nylon and a certain kind of bond against our ruin, fine. Countries are marching on each other every other minute, civilization at large is fighting an endless battle against disorder, I can't even keep the crumbs off my kitchen table for more than twenty minutes; situations change with lightning speed and almost nothing is certain but for the time being, at least, I can hold on because my corner is still here, and if it is blown up or stolen some morning, I will do my best to re-create it.

There is another side to this coin. The writer needs to impose an apparent external order on his situation precisely because the only real order will have to be dredged up from his own inner chaos, and must be self-imposed. In a civilization which is not necessarily going to pay you for sitting down every morning, or even ask you to do it, you have to simulate a regular working circumstance. External order, or the appearance of external order gives the writer the illusion that he is doing regular work on a perfectly ordinary day-to-day basis, but there is more to it: this order gives you as writer a more or less secure place to depart from on those forays into what is essentially uncharted territory.

This external order also spares you dozens of petty and unnecessary decisions, any one of which offers a perfect excuse not to work at all. If you always go to work at a certain time then you don't have to sit around trying to decide when to work, which eliminates one of your last remaining excuses. If you always stop work at more or less the same time every day, then you don't have to figure out when to stop or worry about whether you've done enough for the day. If the day's output turns out to be one sentence that satisfies you, that's fine. If a scene of several pages takes you by surprise, that's fine. In either case you will know when to stop because the allotted time has passed and it's time to stop. If you always type, or always compose in longhand, or always use a certain kind of paper, then you don't have to figure out what means you're going to use this time around or what your materials are going to be, and you won't have to make a trip across town to get a certain kind of paper that strikes your fancy. If you always work in the same place you are not going to get hung up on whether it's the library you're going to use to court inspiration or whether you're going to hang out in an empty classroom or try long-distance walking with a pad and pencil or sitting around on rocks. You won't excuse yourself from work that day because you aren't in the mood. Moods are immaterial. Real writers don't wait for inspiration or stop and ask whether they feel like working that day; they simply go to the desk, wherever it is, and get started.

If you want to be a writer, sooner or later you have to sit down and write. Even if you have established a schedule which deposits you at your desk at the same hour every day, you will have to begin again. If you become a writer, this is an act of will you have to make every day of your working life, and I can report that it never gets much easier.

Some writers find letter writing helps to break the ice. It puts you in the right place at the right time going through the right motions and the leap from letter writing into the day's work is not as formidable as that initial plunge.

Other writers will go over their notes or rework yesterday's pages, editing copy or retyping. I usually start at the top of my chapter file and rework on the computer screen, which serves two functions: it joins yesterday's work to to-day's so there are no seams showing, and it gives me a certain momentum, so that by the time I reach the great empty spaces at the end of yesterday's work, I can keep going. If I manage to do it right, working faster and faster, I can sneak up on the new work and pounce.

Even writers who have published several stories or novels will wake up on certain mornings with no work in progress and nothing planned. Unless they plan to give it up and go out to lunch for the rest of their lives, they will resort to some of the processes available to beginning writers.

Many writers use the notebook. Some writers keep notes all their lives, recording observations, good lines overheard in restaurants, isolated sentences that pop into their heads. For them this is another form of collecting. The notes are like money in the bank, to be drawn on in dry periods. Sometimes the notes will sit for years until one of them begins compounding and beomes a story or a novel.

Others of us use the notebook differently, in a kind of Monday-morning desperation, sketching at random or noodling the way a pianist does, striking occasional notes until a pattern emerges and the pattern becomes a melody. We will write down locations, names of people, bits of the past, projections, making fitful lines or daggers in the margins and then, at some unidentifiable moment, writing more and more under one of the entries until it becomes apparent that there is a story.

Another starting point for some writers is the journal, in which the journal-ist begins to shape experience. As you put down the events of the day you are going to have to make choices about what to put in and what to leave out, which parts are worth giving more time and space to, how to write about what has happened. This is not an absolute account of a given day; it is an account of a given day already shaped and filtered through the writer's consciousness. Going back to the journal a few days or weeks later, you will look at the account of that particular day and remember what you have chosen to remember. This in part determines the shape of any story you may make out of the raw material you have in front of you.

These methods all have the virtue of involving the physical act of writing, and if it's possible to sneak up on a story when it isn't looking, putting words on paper may help. You may think you think better while sitting under a tree or riding a bicycle and if this is true, then by all means do whatever seems right to you. The truth is that there are probably as many methods of discovering stories as there are stories waiting to be written, that none of them can ensure success and maybe half the ideas that come to you will be useless, but the inescapable fact is that stories won't come at all unless you invite them. Whether you begin by spinning out ideas on a long walk or in a semiconscious state while lying on the sofa or staring out the window or taking hot baths or doing yoga, you are going to end up back at your desk sooner or later because this is where the process completes itself.

With the times set aside and the place settled on, and something to write about, you have eliminated your last remaining excuse. It's time to begin. In order to begin, you have to know what you're going to write about this time around, and I can report that this part never gets any easier. Sometimes the only thing that keeps a writer going is the knowledge that it happened here before, in these circumstances, it has happened lots of times, which means that sooner or later, it is going to happen again. On the other hand the idea, or whatever it was, may leave without you if you aren't around to seize it as it goes by. Here comes . . . there goes . . . something wonderful I was going to write about. Hence office hours, office procedures.

Once you are in the place where you write at the time you usually sit down to write, there are any number of devices for getting started, from note transcribing to letter writing to window-shade-adjusting or pacing or pressing your face against the glass just one more time to be absolutely sure the mailman hasn't come while you weren't looking. There are times when the state approaches desperation, and at those times the familiar old desk or table is strangely comforting.

If you have work left over from yesterday, it's useful to begin by reading it through, looking at possibilities for revision. With subtle word alterations, the meaning clarifies; it's a little like the steps a diver takes before plunging.

If you work on the typewriter you may want to try retyping or you may want to do what many writers do, proofreading yesterday's work, making changes in pen or pencil. The function in any case is to join yesterday's work to today's without any visible seams. If there's nothing left over from yesterday, you may want to start with a few lines of dialog or by throwing yourself at a first sentence, casting and recasting until it seems right and a story begins to develop.

If you're writing by hand it's a good idea to skip every other line on the pad so there will be room for revisions. At a certain point your first draft will be so tracked with corrections that you'll know it's time to copy it over. Messy pages make sense for a limited amount of time; sooner or later the mess takes over. This is another example of external order serving the order of the work;

if you can see what you are doing, you'll be able to do it better, and you'll probably find that the work clarifies itself in the recopying. If you're composing on the typewriter or computer, double or triple space for the same reason. Any typing or retyping you do will supply considerably more than external order. If you think you might be famous, save these working papers, because some friendly library may be thrilled to preserve them, and if the law changes you can deduct the appraised value from your taxable income.

If you write for long enough, and work hard enough at it, you will eventually have a manuscript you think is finished and ready to offer to editors. When you submit your manuscript be sure it is typed, double spaced, and carefully proofread before it leaves your hands. Type only on one side of the paper. Put your name and address on the title page and on either the first or the last page of the copy as well. To avoid losses, use a staple. Paper clips slip and make the top page look messy. If you are submitting your story to a magazine, enclose a stamped, self-addressed envelope. It's better to send your story in an envelope large enough to permit the manuscript to stay flat. If it returns to you in a dog-eared state, retype the title page before sending it on to the next place so the story won't look used. Most editors want to believe they are the first to see a given story.

If you have published anything else, it may be useful to let the editor know what and where in a short cover letter. Literary or "little" magazines can take from three to six months to get around to reporting on a story. I think it's all right to jog editors after, say, two months. ("Dear editor, two months ago I sent you my story, VAIN WHEAT, and so far I have had no word about it. I am writing to be sure it was not lost in transit . . .")

Chances are it was not lost in the mail. If it was, you will hear about it. If you send a stamped, self-addressed postcard with your query you will find out whether your story has been lost or whether it has been lying forgotten in somebody's bottom drawer or whether the magazine is, in fact, considering it seriously. The query may dislodge it. Mass-circulation magazines are usually more efficient, but if you pass the two-month mark without hearing, it won't hurt to send a similar query.

If you're worried about your manuscript's arriving safely, you can enclose a stamped self-addressed postcard acknowledging receipt. Professionals won't usually bother with registered or certified mail unless they're submitting book-length manuscripts (one magazine editor pointed out to me that receipt requested situations give him a chance to refuse delivery), but have been known to use express mail for rhetorical effect. It's an expensive habit, but guarantees delivery, and next-day delivery. Better not fax a manuscript unless an editor has asked you to.

It is wise to mail stories in batches, one each to several different magazines, instead of pinning all your hopes on one story. Then if one comes back, it isn't the end of everything. You mail it to another magazine as quickly as possible, before one of the other stories bounces. It's a little like juggling oranges; if they all land on your head at once, you'll probably give up juggling, but if you can keep at least two or three in the air, the one that drops and splatters won't be so depressing. If you get a handwritten line on the bottom of the usual printed rejection slip, it means the editor is interested in you and you should keep trying that magazine. If you get a full letter from an editor the next time out, chances are you're in business.

Keep a notebook with a page for expenses incurred in buying supplies and mailing, and one page for each story. Note down the date each one is sent and where, and when it is returned, so that no editor has two stories of yours at the same time and you don't send the same story twice to the same editor. Never submit a story to more than one publication at a time; most editors expect single submissions.

If you begin to sell your work, the expense items in your notebook will become important, as they will be tax deductible, along with postage, duplication costs and the appropriate percentage of heat, electricity and rent for the room in which you write if you work at home and don't use the room for anything else. Later on you will be able to depreciate your professional library and your typewriter.

I don't think as beginning writer you need an agent until you've published something. Until you have published, you are going to find it difficult to interest a reputable agent, although most are generous about looking at work by new writers. Incidentally, a reputable agent will not charge for a reading. There are certain agencies which advertise reading services for a fee. I suspect the back room is filled with exhausted peons with red pencils, all of them prepared to give the would-be writer anything from a superficial response for $5 to a deep analysis for $25 — with higher rates for your novel. Like vanity presses, they survive on your money. As a professional writer, you should not have to pay to have your work read, or, indeed, pay to have it published.

A different kind of organization is the Scott Meredith agency, which combines standard operations with clients as well-known as Norman Mailer with a read-for-pay operation. A Florida writer who had received one of Meredith's brochures took on the agency in a letter to *The New York Times Book Review*. He suggested delicately that he was charmed that Meredith's office might be interested in reading his work (on payment of a fee) but he felt the shoe should be on the other foot and he would forward his work as soon as Mr. Meredith sent the $150 check he thought was appropriate for a look at his new novel.

As a beginner, you can go a considerable distance by yourself. Literary or "little" magazines are used to dealing directly with authors, as are many of the pulps and smaller mass-circulation magazines. There are magazines and yearbooks listing potential markets, with names of who to write to, which places will accept unsolicited manuscripts and other information. Many publishers still have some faith in the chance that they will find hidden treasure and therefore will look at unsolicited first novels. Some even have competitions to encourage new talent. Even those who don't will respond to a query letter and may be willing to look at a chapter and an outline.

If you have managed to place one or two stories or have distinguished yourself in some other way, by editing the college literary magazine or winning prizes for writing, you may be ready to look for an agent. If you have been writing regularly and sending out stories, you'll probably have at least a writing acquaintance with one or two editors, perhaps another writer or two, and they may be able to advise you as to where to begin looking for an agent. If you are studying with a teacher who is also a writer or have been in a writing workshop conducted by one or another writer, you may be able to approach an agent through that writer. If you haven't any contacts and have no idea where to begin you can obtain a list of agents from the Society of Authors' Representatives, which is headquartered in New York. The society offers a brochure listing members and telling beginning writers what to look for and how to proceed in locating an agent.

Instead of kiting in a manuscript and expecting an agent to give it a reading simply because you've asked for one, write a query letter. It's perfectly all right to send it to several agents at the same time. Make your letter short and interesting enough to get a stranger's attention, remembering that agents, like publishers, still hope to unearth buried treasure. List the places you've published, describe what you have in hand and ask for a reading. An agent can get your work read at publications like *Esquire* and *Harper's Magazine* that automatically return unsolicited manuscripts. Although most agents will handle short fiction, some only do so for successful or long-established clients. You'll find out by querying.

Don't expect to sell something the first time out or the second or even the twentieth time out. Think of the submissions as part of the learning process. You are getting some indication of how the world at large responds to your work and you are, by the simple act of living through the first rejection slip and the next, and the next, getting tougher. Don't try to guess how long it will take you to sell the first story and don't tell yourself that the first sale is going to herald anything more than the first sale, any more than you're going to tell yourself that your first novel is going to make you famous. That's not the name of the game.

Making a career as a writer is going to take longer than you think and it's going to be much harder than you could ever predict. If you knew now how long it was going to take or how hard it was going to be you would probably give up in despair. It's better not to try and guess the future. Concentrate on elements you think you can control: the setting, the method, the work itself. It is in the work that you will find the most pleasure.

If you're a smoker, it's a good idea to separate smoking from working right at the outset. I have one playwright friend who spent unhappy months after he quit smoking before he could work without a cigarette. My friend the composer can't quit smoking even though his lungs are rotting and his teeth loosening because he has enough problems getting to work as it is, and he can't work without smoking. I suspect the same advice would extend to working while high on anything. Whatever it is, save it until you don't need it. If you have to smoke or drink, do it after work. It's a bad idea to incorporate outside props into working patterns.

I have saved what may be the most important advice for last. Never let a manuscript leave the house without having an extra copy in your own hands. Even if you feel foolish doing it, duplicate everything you send out, even if it's only a couple of pages. I have gone through entire garbage cans to retrieve a single lost page, scraping off whatever was stuck to it because no matter how nasty that was, it was nicer than trying to re-create it. I will extend this even farther. If you're writing a novel, have the manuscript duplicated every hundred pages or so, and keep the second copy somewhere else.

If you're working on a computer with a hard disk, back up everything you write on floppies and keep the backups in a safe place because hard disks of a certain age have been known to crash and you can't afford to gamble on what age that is. Whether or not you print out every day, print out at the end of every story or, in the case of a novel, at the end of every chapter. If you work only on floppies, back your files up regularly. You'll want to make a backup disk in addition to the disk you're working on and keep it in a safe place, partly for insurance against fire, flood, or theft and partly because even the best floppies have been known to crash mysteriously.

Terrible things happen to writers who don't keep copies of their work. Cases in point: it's possible that we would have read Ralph Ellison's second novel by now if his house hadn't burned down several years ago with most of his working papers in it. Kay Boyle had the first four chapters of her monumental and perhaps perpetually unfinished history of Germany stolen out of her car by some junkie who liked the look of her attaché case. By now everybody knows what happened to the first copy of Carlyle's *The French Revolution*. If you are called away unexpectedly you can put the manuscript into the deep-freeze or the hydrator pan of the refrigerator, and you may feel like an anxious fool doing it but I can tell you that anything is better than trying to catch the style and spirit of a work that has escaped you.

People say to me, "I don't know how you do all the things you do," and, "you're so *disciplined*," and they don't always mean it kindly. The first is true because of the second, and the second is true for all the reasons I have outlined. There is, of course, that underlying reason: whatever it is in my history and makeup that makes me a writer. Without reference to this I manage to look composed and seem capable, so the people who ask the questions will never find out the truth from me: the external order is all those things I said it was, and more. It is working for me all the time, it's working for me now; it is, quite simply, another of those things a writer does to keep from going crazy.

15

DISCIPLINE

*N*ow we have arrived at the question I tactfully left for last: whether you will ever be a writer. Even passing by at a dead gallop, I can look at a group of student writers and tell you which ones have gifts: real talent. But if I slow down to ask questions, even after long, careful looks into each one's eyes, I cannot tell you which, if any, are going to be writers.

The extraordinary truth is that all those gifts: facility with language and ideas, a dramatic sense, even occasional flashes of brilliance, are nothing more than superficial assets. As the casting director said to the dancing Amazon who also played the slide trombone, OK, sweetie, what else did you bring?

The invisible but essential rest of the package is a combination of compulsion, endurance and sustained discipline, coupled with a toughness necessary for survival. Once these have been numbered there is still the imponderable: what makes the artist. Wanting to be helpful, trying to make a definition for you or set down a few directions, I find I cannot separate gifts and drive from discipline and even if I did there would still be that imponderable remaining, something as difficult to sort out for scrutiny as the human soul. I suspect that there is a link between this unknown quality and survival; I am willing to guess that what makes the artist also makes that artist persist beyond the point at which less gifted and driven people understand at last that they are neither of those things and simply stop writing.

The compulsion to make fiction is innate. The toughness is of necessity developed over the years because a writer of fiction is selling himself in certain mysterious ways, and those refusals of stories and novels are at least in part refusals of that self. If you are going to persist, understand that there are people in hobnailed boots standing in line for the privilege of trampling the white flowers of your imagination.

If it is the imponderable that makes you survive, the instrument is easier to identify. It is discipline. I can't say that discipline makes the artist but you will never be an artist without discipline.

There is no way to impose discipline from the outside or explain it to somebody who does not have it. Discipline is the willingness to get on with it, and on and on with it, through depression and pain and beyond exhaustion, to do whatever is necessary to accomplish that which you set out to accomplish.

Discipline comes with time. It must be developed, served and maintained through good times and bad. Once it is established, it is self-serving. It is, in part, its own reward, which makes it just about as seductive and rewarding as virtue: the results are only visible in the long run. It is a necessary tool which survives disappointment, outlasts inspiration and keeps the work going even when there are no immediate rewards and no rewards in sight. You must work for it if you ever hope to be a writer.

Being a writer means keeping regular office hours when there is no boss watching, more: it means keeping regular office hours under a certain emotional stress to create a product for which there is no immediate demand and for which there may not be a market. Worse yet, it means keeping these hours under this stress to create this unwanted product, while at the same time maintaining rigid quality control according to exacting, often elusive inner standards, and finishing a piece of work according to these standards to discover that you, the writer, are the only human being who admires it.

It takes more than talent to do that. For some, I think, discipline comes first and the gifts develop and emerge only with time, a partial payoff for the years of dedication. For others, whose gifts are apparent from the beginning, the perfection of the gifts will come only after years of close and demanding work. For the talented, writing begins by being easy; with the exercise of discipline, it is harder and harder. The rewards are not necessarily immediate, but the punishment, if that's what it is, is apparent. Unused, talents atrophy.

Perhaps because I am a collector at heart, my mind is littered with unfinished novels: other people's.

There was the acquaintance who broke up her marriage in order to develop her talent as a writer. She was writing a novel about her busted marriage, and because she had made a few literary contacts, she had a major publisher looking interested and some would-be fans at *The New York Review of Books*. At least she said she did. The only thing is, it's been several years now, and there still isn't any novel.

There was the college senior whose first novel was optioned by a publisher on the basis of Part I, which he had written under supervision, which meant a certain degree of discipline, externally imposed. Then he finished college and had to write Part II all by himself, which he finally got around to, doing a slapdash, half-hearted version which the publisher, naturally, refused. Now he says he's dying to rewrite the second half, but he doesn't want to do it until somebody promises to publish it. In short, he wants a guaranteed market in a business where that seldom happens. He has a classmate who wasn't satisfied with his first novel, wrote a second and had it published, to considerable success. Discipline? Discipline.

There is the lady down the block who ditched her family so she could write a novel. I'm afraid to ask how it's going. The last thing I heard, she had plenty of raw material but said she was having trouble with the style.

There is the occasional friend who wants me to collaborate on a novel: he'll supply the material because he has this truly fabulous idea and all this inside dope, all I have to do is put it into shape. I don't have to tell him I'd rather die. All I have to do is say, "Why don't you work up a ten-page outline, and then we'll talk." I am perfectly safe because the friend is not a writer, will never be, and because that friend will never take the first step, I am spared the necessity of refusing.

Somebody we knew in college took up cod fishing off the Cape so he could write the Great American Novel in his spare time. Spare time is not when Great American Novels get written. It's been years now, and we are going to have to conclude that he's probably spying on Russian trawlers instead. They may not be out there any more, but *he* is.

Last week I read an academic job application by somebody who wrote that he was writing a novel. Because I believe almost everything people tell me, I was impressed. How exciting, he's writing a novel, isn't that wonderful. Then I thought: hey, wait a minute, anybody can *say* he's writing a novel. It's just like my friend Dopey who said she had a miniature village in her attic; as long as nobody got into her attic to see it firsthand, it could be true.

This was last week. It seems to have taken me all these years to make a final distinction between people who say they are writers and people who are writers.

People who are writers get it written, and when it's published you get a copy of it. If it isn't published, you don't hear about it, except in passing. Somebody may admit he has a busted novel; it's a little like having a miscarriage. More often than not, real writers won't talk about work in progress, perhaps because their storerooms, like mine, are littered with the corpses of great unwritten novels: other people's. There is, furthermore, the writer's superstition which may be, rather, actual folk knowledge. If you talk it through, or tell somebody else too much about it, you are going to use it all up, no matter how good it is, before you ever get it onto paper.

What cuts the line between all those great unwritten novels and actual acts of fiction is discipline.

Discipline keeps the writer doing what needs doing. It gets books written, perfected, published. It is among other things a process of distillation which forges ideas from rough beginnings and realizes them in prose which is worked and reworked until it says precisely what the writer intends. Discipline means being willing to grapple with a passage until you have narrowed the gap between intention and execution: once more through the typewriter. Now: again, Again. It involves rough drafts and final drafts, page drafts and sentence drafts, bits of scrap paper filled with possible word choices, a certain measure of distraction when the rest of the world expects you to be paying attention to something else. It also involves a willingness to listen to useful criticism and an instinctive hardening of the will against criticism which seems reasonable but which is wrong because it is aimed at making the work more popular in appeal instead of making it come out *right*. You have to be willing to admit that nothing you write is ever perfect and be willing to face the fact that there may be ways to improve it, but this knowledge has to be coupled with an integrity that rules out compromise for the sake of compromise.

For the writer, discipline is complex. Understanding all of the above, you have to be willing to go to the desk when your mind is empty and your mood desperate, and you have to be willing to stay there, staring out the window or picking at your typewriter keys with a straight pin or using any one of a dozen other devices, playing at work without anything to show for it, until the real work presents itself. You must be willing to try out solution after solution, grappling with a particular artistic problem until the right solution emerges, and you have to be able to reject all those wrong solutions which come so easily, keeping the mind open even if it's days, or weeks, before the problem solves itself and the work flows as it should.

Discipline means being bored, at least part of the time, because the work is elusive.

It means doing something hard even when you don't feel like it.

Finally, discipline is a matter of refusing to quit. You may threaten to abandon the typewriter or sell the computer and take up a regular job: garbage collecting, ditch digging, one of any number of more rewarding pursuits, but once the discipline is there, it takes charge. Once you are a writer you will never quit because nothing else will satisfy you.

It is discipline which separates the real writer from all those well-meaning people who think they would write terrific fiction if only they had enough spare time.

I will not attempt to catalog for you the accumulated hundreds of years of work, the dozens of busted novels, the scores of disappointments logged by the small handful of writers I know personally; I will only say that it takes all those years of work and a fair share of those disappointments to make any well-intentioned person of talent into a writer, and that in the final analysis the rewards don't come after the fact of the work, in the form of friends, money, fame, or even in the completed piece of fiction but in the work itself: all that gruelling process.

Maybe it's easier to be, instead, the author of one of those great unfinished novels. So long as you haven't finished a novel, you'll never have to find out whether it's publishable. If it isn't published, you'll never have to find out whether anybody wants to read it, whether booksellers will handle it, whether reviewers will write about it, whether anybody is even going to like it. In a way, the work still exists, perfect and untried, inside the mind, glittering like any grail. In the long run, what's the matter with keeping it there?

As the author of a great unfinished novel, you have some of the cachet with none of the attendant pain. People will regard you with respect. How about that. This person is a *writer*. Once you have published, no matter how good your work is, some jerk is going to come along and say, "That's all very well, but I didn't care much for your book." It's cozier to let your works linger in what my resident critic calls the vestibule of the uncreated. Your works can be untouched, just about as real as Dopey's village. So long as you don't let anybody in to see your works, you'll never have to test them. As one of my characters keeps saying, "Unless you lay it on the line, nobody's going to come along and cut it off."

Furthermore, as author of the great unfinished novel, you can maintain the perfection of a vision which is always flawed by realization. An idea is at its most promising when it is shimmering out there in the middle distance. Once it takes flesh there are all those missteps and unbidden changes which creep in because the work will always fall short of the vision.

If imagined or projected works appeal to you: perfect because unrealized, safe, then keep them in the imagination. You will never be a writer.

For the real writer, this gap between intention and realization is a recognized part of the process, and what keeps the writer going is that next vision, shimmering just out of reach. None of us is ever going to reach perfection, but with time we may come a little closer, and the possibility keeps us going through this piece of work to the next and the next and the one after. I spent the better part of one dinner-table conversation defending the right of one artist friend to abandon safe work, simple successes, in pursuit of the vision. She kept tripping over things and making messes in search of a new method of expression but she was in there trying. After a while it is the aspiration, or pursuit, which becomes important, which is probably a damn good thing, because there aren't any immediate rewards, either in terms of what the work becomes, or what it brings you: friends, money, fame, because no matter what the world brings you, it will never be enough. As another of my characters keeps saying:

UNLESS YOU AIM HIGH YOU'LL NEVER FALL SHORT

If you don't know what that means, you'll never be a writer.

Index

Other Books of Interest

Annual Market Books

Artist's Market, edited by Lauri Miller $21.95

Children's Writer's & Illustrator's Market, edited by Lisa Carpenter (paper) $16.95

Guide to Literary Agents & Art/Photo Reps, edited by Robin Gee $15.95

Humor & Cartoon Markets, edited by Bob Staake (paper) $16.95

Novel & Short Story Writer's Market, edited by Robin Gee (paper) $18.95

Photographer's Market, edited by Sam Marshall $21.95

Poet's Market, by Judson Jerome $19.95

Songwriter's Market, edited by Brian Rushing $19.95

Writer's Market, edited by Mark Kissling $25.95

General Writing Books

Annable's Treasury of Literary Teasers, by H.D. Annable (paper) $10.95

Beginning Writer's Answer Book, edited by Kirk Polking (paper) $13.95

Discovering the Writer Within, by Bruce Ballenger & Barry Lane $16.95

Getting the Words Right: How to Rewrite, Edit and Revise, by Theodore A. Rees Cheney (paper) $12.95

How to Write a Book Proposal, by Michael Larsen (paper) $10.95

Just Open a Vein, edited by William Brohaugh $15.95

Knowing Where to Look: The Ultimate Guide to Research, by Lois Horowitz (paper) $16.95

Make Your Words Work, by Gary Provost $17.95

On Being a Writer, edited by Bill Strickland $19.95

Pinckert's Practical Grammar, by Robert C. Pinckert (paper) $11.95

The Story Behind the Word, by Morton S. Freeman (paper) $9.95

12 Keys to Writing Books That Sell, by Kathleen Krull (paper) $12.95

The 29 Most Common Writing Mistakes & How to Avoid Them, by Judy Delton (paper) $9.95

The Wordwatcher's Guide to Good Writing & Grammar, by Morton S. Freeman (paper) $15.95

Word Processing Secrets for Writers, by Michael A. Banks & Ansen Dibell (paper) $14.95

The Writer's Book of Checklists, by Scott Edelstein $16.95

The Writer's Digest Guide to Manuscript Formats, by Buchman & Groves $18.95

The Writer's Essential Desk Reference, edited by Glenda Neff $19.95

Nonfiction Writing

The Complete Guide to Writing Biographies, by Ted Schwarz $19.95

Creative Conversations: The Writer's Guide to Conducting Interviews, by Michael Schumacher $16.95

How to Do Leaflets, Newsletters, & Newspapers, by Nancy Brigham (paper) $14.95

How to Sell Every Magazine Article You Write, by Lisa Collier Cool (paper) $11.95

How to Write Irresistible Query Letters, by Lisa Collier Cool (paper) $10.95

The Writer's Digest Handbook of Magazine Article Writing, edited by Jean M. Fredette (paper) $11.95

Fiction Writing

The Art & Craft of Novel Writing, by Oakley Hall $17.95

Best Stories from New Writers, edited by Linda Sanders $16.95

Characters & Viewpoint, by Orson Scott Card $13.95

The Complete Guide to Writing Fiction, by Barnaby Conrad $17.95

Cosmic Critiques: How & Why 10 Science Fiction Stories Work, edited by Asimov & Greenberg (paper) $12.95

Creating Characters: How to Build Story People, by Dwight V. Swain $16.95

Creating Short Fiction, by Damon Knight (paper) $10.95

Dare to Be a Great Writer: 329 Keys to Powerful Fiction, by Leonard Bishop $16.95

Dialogue, by Lewis Turco $13.95

The Fiction Writer's Silent Partner, by Martin Roth $19.95

Handbook of Short Story Writing: Vol. I, by Dickson and Smythe (paper) $10.95

Handbook of Short Story Writing: Vol. II, edited by Jean Fredette (paper) $12.95

How to Write & Sell Your First Novel, by Collier & Leighton (paper) $12.95

Manuscript Submission, by Scott Edelstein $13.95

Mastering Fiction Writing, by Kit Reed $18.95

Plot, by Ansen Dibell $13.95

Revision, by Kit Reed $13.95

Spider Spin Me a Web: Lawrence Block on Writing Fiction, by Lawrence Block $16.95

Theme & Strategy, by Ronald B. Tobias $13.95

Writing the Novel: From Plot to Print, by Lawrence Block (paper) $10.95

Special Interest Writing Books

Armed & Dangerous: A Writer's Guide to Weapons, by Michael Newton (paper) $14.95

The Children's Picture Book: How to Write It, How to Sell It, by Ellen E.M. Roberts (paper) $18.95

The Complete Book of Feature Writing, by Leonard Witt $18.95

The Complete Book of Scriptwriting, by J. Michael Straczynski (paper) $11.95

Creating Poetry, by John Drury $18.95

Deadly Doses: A Writer's Guide to Poisons, by Serita Deborah Stevens with Anne Klarner (paper) $16.95

Editing Your Newsletter, by Mark Beach (paper) $18.50

Families Writing, by Peter Stillman $15.95

A Guide to Travel Writing & Photography, by Ann & Carl Purcell (paper) $22.95

Hillary Waugh's Guide to Mysteries & Mystery Writing, by Hillary Waugh $19.95

How to Pitch & Sell Your TV Script, by David Silver $17.95

How to Write a Play, by Raymond Hull (paper) $12.95

How to Write Action/Adventure Novels, by Michael Newton $13.95

How to Write & Sell True Crime, by Gary Provost $17.95

How to Write Horror Fiction, by William F. Nolan $15.95

How to Write Mysteries, by Shannon OCork $13.95

How to Write Romances, by Phyllis Taylor Pianka $13.95

How to Write Science Fiction & Fantasy, by Orson Scott Card $13.95

How to Write Tales of Horror, Fantasy & Science Fiction, edited by J.N. Williamson (paper) $12.95

How to Write the Story of Your Life, by Frank P. Thomas (paper) $11.95

How to Write Western Novels, by Matt Braun $13.95

The Magazine Article: How To Think It, Plan It, Write It, by Peter Jacobi $17.95

Mystery Writer's Handbook, by The Mystery Writers of America (paper) $11.95

The Poet's Handbook, by Judson Jerome (paper) $10.95

Successful Scriptwriting, by Jurgen Wolff & Kerry Cox (paper) $14.95

TV Scriptwriter's Handbook, by Alfred Brenner (paper) $10.95

The Writer's Complete Crime Reference Book, by Martin Roth $19.95

The Writer's Guide to Conquering the Magazine Market, by Connie Emerson $17.95

Writing for Children & Teenagers, 3rd Edition, by Lee Wyndham & Arnold Madison (paper) $12.95

Writing the Modern Mystery, by Barbara Norville $15.95

Writing to Inspire, edited by William Gentz (paper) $14.95

The Writing Business

A Beginner's Guide to Getting Published, edited by Kirk Polking (paper) $11.95

The Complete Guide to Self-Publishing, by Tom & Marilyn Ross (paper) $16.95

How to Write with a Collaborator, by Hal Bennett with Michael Larsen $11.95

How You Can Make $25,000 a Year Writing, by Nancy Edmonds Hanson (paper) $12.95

Is There a Speech Inside You?, by Don Aslett (paper) $9.95

Time Management for Writers, by Ted Schwarz $10.95

The Writer's Friendly Legal Guide, edited by Kirk Polking $16.95

Writer's Guide to Self-Promotion & Publicity, by Elane Feldman $16.95

A Writer's Guide to Contract Negotiations, by Richard Balkin (paper) $11.95

Writing A to Z, edited by Kirk Polking $22.95

To order directly from the publisher, include $3.00 postage and handling for 1 book and $1.00 for each additional book. Allow 30 days for delivery.

Writer's Digest Books

1507 Dana Avenue, Cincinnati, Ohio 45207

Credit card orders call TOLL-FREE

1-800-289-0963

Prices subject to change without notice.

Write to this same address for information on *Writer's Digest* magazine, *Story* magazine, Writer's Digest Book Club, Writer's Digest School, and Writer's Digest Criticism Service.